HISTORY

RECLAIMING THE
CHRISTIAN INTELLECTUAL TRADITION

David S. Dockery, series editor

CONSULTING EDITORS

Hunter Baker
Timothy George
Niel Nielson
Philip G. Ryken
Michael J. Wilkins
John D. Woodbridge

OTHER RCIT VOLUMES:

The Great Tradition of Christian Thinking, David S. Dockery and
    Timothy George
The Liberal Arts, Gene C. Fant Jr.
Political Thought, Hunter Baker
Literature, Louis Markos
Philosophy, David K. Naugle
Christian Worldview, Philip G. Ryken
Art and Music, Paul Munson and Joshua Farris Drake
Ethics and Moral Reasoning, C. Ben Mitchell

"I heartily recommend Nathan Finn's brisk and thoughtful *History: A Student's Guide*. I do not know of a better introduction to historical studies, or a more cogent assessment of how Christians should think about history."

Thomas S. Kidd, Professor of History, Baylor University; author, *The Great Awakening: The Roots of Evangelical Christianity in Colonial America*

"Nathan Finn's adept introduction to the art and discipline of history and historical scholarship will provide many students, especially those with explicit faith commitments, with the resources needed to participate in the ongoing conversations of the guild."

Richard A. Bailey, Associate Professor of History, Canisius College; author, *Race and Redemption in Puritan New England*

"This mature, thorough, and insightful Christian treatment of history and the historian's craft will prove to be an indispensable tool for students. In this concise and engaging book, Nathan Finn employs characteristic wit and wisdom as he guides his readers through the essentials of understanding the 'foreign country' of the past. Here's a book every aspiring historian must read."

John D. Wilsey, Assistant Professor of History and Christian Apologetics, Southwestern Baptist Theological Seminary; author, *American Exceptionalism* and *Civil Religion*

"Nathan Finn has contributed an excellent resource for introducing students to the essential principles and responsible practice of historical studies from a Christian perspective. The text is filled with colorful illustrations from contemporary popular culture that give it a timely relevance while also containing loads of timeless wisdom. *History: A Student's Guide* deserves a long tenure as an essential text for Christian reflections on the nature and doing of history."

Scott Culpepper, Associate Professor of History, Dordt College

HISTORY
A STUDENT'S
GUIDE

Nathan A. Finn

WHEATON, ILLINOIS

History: A Student's Guide

Copyright © 2016 by Nathan A. Finn

Published by Crossway
　　　　　1300 Crescent Street
　　　　　Wheaton, Illinois 60187

Cover design: Jon McGrath, Simplicated Studio

First printing 2016

Printed in the United States of America

Trade paperback ISBN: 978-1-4335-3763-9
ePub ISBN: 978-1-4335-3766-0
PDF ISBN: 978-1-4335-3764-6
Mobipocket ISBN: 978-1-4335-3765-3

Library of Congress Cataloging-in-Publication Data

Finn, Nathan A.
　　History : a student's guide / Nathan A. Finn.
　　　　pages cm.— (Reclaiming the Christian intellectual tradition)
　　　　Includes bibliographical references and index.
　　　　ISBN 978-1-4335-3763-9 (tp)
　　　　1. History—Religious aspects—Christianity. I. Title.
BR115.H5F475　　　　2016
261.5—dc23　　　　　　　　　　　　　　　　　　　2015020204

Crossway is a publishing ministry of Good News Publishers.

VP		26	25	24	23	22	21	20	19	18	17	16
15	14	13	12	11	10	9	8	7	6	5	4	3	2	1

For my beloved wife,
Leah Phillips Finn
You have walked with me
and encouraged me
and challenged me
and supported me
and, most important, loved me
as I have pursued the vocation
of Christian historian.

CONTENTS

SERIES PREFACE

The Reclaiming the Christian Intellectual Tradition series is designed to provide an overview of the distinctive way the church has read the Bible, formulated doctrine, provided education, and engaged the culture. The contributors to this series all agree that personal faith and genuine Christian piety are essential for the life of Christ followers and for the church. These contributors also believe that helping others recognize the importance of serious thinking about God, Scripture, and the world needs a renewed emphasis at this time in order that the truth claims of the Christian faith can be passed along from one generation to the next. The study guides in this series will enable us to see afresh how the Christian faith shapes how we live, how we think, how we write books, how we govern society, and how we relate to one another in our churches and social structures. The richness of the Christian intellectual tradition provides guidance for the complex challenges that believers face in this world.

This series is particularly designed for Christian students and others associated with college and university campuses, including faculty, staff, trustees, and other various constituents. The contributors to the series will explore how the Bible has been interpreted in the history of the church, as well as how theology has been formulated. They will ask: How does the Christian faith influence our understanding of culture, literature, philosophy, government, beauty, art, or work? How does the Christian intellectual tradition help us understand truth? How does the Christian intellectual tradition shape our approach to education? We believe that this series is not only timely but that it meets an important need, because the secular culture in which we now find ourselves is, at best, indifferent to the Christian faith, and the Christian world—at least in its more popular forms—tends to be confused about the beliefs, heritage, and tradition associated with the Christian faith.

At the heart of this work is the challenge to prepare a generation of Christians to think Christianly, to engage the academy and the culture, and to serve church and society. We believe that both the breadth and the depth of the Christian intellectual tradition need to be reclaimed, revitalized, renewed, and revived for us to carry this work forward. These study guides will seek to provide a framework to help introduce students to the great tradition of Christian thinking, seeking to highlight its importance for understanding the world, its significance for serving both church and society, and its application for Christian thinking and learning. The series is a starting point for exploring important ideas and issues such as truth, meaning, beauty, and justice.

We trust that the series will help introduce readers to the apostles, church fathers, Reformers, philosophers, theologians, historians, and a wide variety of other significant thinkers. In addition to well-known leaders such as Clement, Origen, Augustine, Thomas Aquinas, Martin Luther, and Jonathan Edwards, readers will be pointed to William Wilberforce, G. K. Chesterton, T. S. Eliot, Dorothy Sayers, C. S. Lewis, Johann Sebastian Bach, Isaac Newton, Johannes Kepler, George Washington Carver, Elizabeth Fox-Genovese, Michael Polanyi, Henry Luke Orombi, and many others. In doing so, we hope to introduce those who throughout history have demonstrated that it is indeed possible to be serious about the life of the mind while simultaneously being deeply committed Christians. These efforts to strengthen serious Christian thinking and scholarship will not be limited to the study of theology, scriptural interpretation, or philosophy, even though these areas provide the framework for understanding the Christian faith for all other areas of exploration. In order for us to reclaim and advance the Christian intellectual tradition, we must have some understanding of the tradition itself. The volumes in this series seek to explore this tradition and its application for our twenty-first-century world. Each volume contains a glossary, study questions, and a list of resources for further study, which we trust will provide helpful guidance for our readers.

I am deeply grateful to the series editorial committee: Timothy George, John Woodbridge, Michael Wilkins, Niel Nielson, Philip Ryken, and Hunter Baker. Each of these colleagues joins me in thanking our various contributors for their fine work. We all express our appreciation to Justin Taylor, Jill Carter, Allan Fisher, Lane Dennis, and the Crossway team for their enthusiastic support for the project. We offer the project with the hope that students will be helped, faculty and Christian leaders will be encouraged, institutions will be strengthened, churches will be built up, and, ultimately, that God will be glorified.

Soli Deo Gloria
David S. Dockery
Series Editor

ACKNOWLEDGMENTS

Some books are planned years in advance. Others providentially drop into your lap. This book falls into the latter category. I have been reflecting on the material covered in this book for over fifteen years, first as an undergraduate history major, then as a graduate student studying the history of Christianity, and now as a professor who teaches church history to undergraduates and graduate students and historical method and historiography to doctoral students. I have debated these topics with colleagues, taught them to students, and discussed them with my family and close friends. But I never thought I would write this book. I am grateful to David Dockery for his kind invitation to contribute this volume to the Reclaiming the Christian Intellectual Tradition series and to my editors at Crossway for their assistance along the way.

I am also grateful to numerous individuals who have assisted me as I have written this book. David Dockery and Gene Fant, formerly the President and Executive Vice President for Academic Administration at Union University, invited me to spend a sabbatical at Union during the first half of 2014. Most of this book was drafted during those five months in West Tennessee. Justin Taylor is not only one of my editors at Crossway, but he has also been a regular dialog partner for several years on the relationship between faith and history, a topic I discuss at length in chapter 3. Conversations with others over the years have also helped sharpen my thinking in various ways; I am especially grateful to Stephen Eccher, Keith Harper, Michael Haykin, David Hogg, Steve McKinion, Miles Mullin, Steve Weaver, and Ryan West. Several friends and colleagues read an earlier draft of this manuscript and offered suggestions that I am certain have significantly improved the book. I want to thank Richard Bailey, Keith Harper, Tommy Kidd, Danielle Renstrom, and John Wilsey for making this a better book. Of course, any errors and shortcomings that linger on are my own.

Final thanks are due to my wife, Leah, and my four children: Georgia, Baxter, Eleanor, and Fuller. They were flexible enough to relocate to another state for six months and gracious enough to share me with this book and several other writing projects during that time. Once we returned to North Carolina, they were patient with me as I finished this book while also assimilating back into my regular teaching routine and launching a new Center for Spiritual Formation and Evangelical Spirituality at Southeastern Seminary. In reality, though, my thanks to Leah in particular extend back to long before I undertook the actual writing of this book.

Leah, you have been by my side since the earliest days when I first considered pursuing the vocation of Christian historian (remember that conversation at Zaxby's in Vidalia?). While friends and colleagues have come and gone over the years, you have remained my most constant conversation partner on the topics discussed in this book, as well as just about every other topic under the sun. Leah, you have been a blessing to me for every second since I first winked at you in the college cafeteria (everyone knows that wink is why you sat by me that day). I am the historian—and the man—I am today in large part because of you. This is not the first book I have written, nor is it the biggest, but it is the one that encapsulates the heart of my work as a historian more than any other. Thus, it only seems fitting that this book be dedicated to you.

INTRODUCTION: HISTORY AND THE CHRISTIAN WORLDVIEW

Most of all, perhaps, we need intimate knowledge of the past. Not that the past has any magic about it, but because we cannot study the future, and yet need something to set against the present, to remind us that the basic assumptions have been quite different in different periods and that much which seems certain to the uneducated is merely temporary fashion. A man who has lived in many places is not likely to be deceived by the local errors of his native village; the scholar has lived in many times and is therefore in some degree immune from the great cataract of nonsense that pours from the press and the microphone of his own age.[1]

C. S. Lewis

The words quoted above are taken from an address C. S. Lewis first gave in 1949. Lewis was a renowned scholar of medieval literature, a popular Christian apologist, and the author of the beloved Chronicles of Narnia series of children's books. Though he was not a professional historian by training, as both a scholar and a Christian, Lewis understood the importance of the past. The past takes us places. The past provides needed perspective. The past keeps us humble. Lewis prized the past so much that he famously suggested that the reading of old books is preferable to the reading of new books. "It has always therefore been one of my main endeavours as a teacher," Lewis writes, "to persuade the young that firsthand knowledge is not only more worth acquiring than secondhand knowledge,

---

[1] C. S. Lewis, "Learning in War-Time," in *The Weight of Glory: And Other Addresses* (New York: HarperOne, 2001), 58–59.

but is usually much easier and more delightful to acquire."[2] Any historian worth his or her salt would agree.

Unfortunately, not everyone would agree that knowledge of the past is valuable—or at least interesting. I have taught history courses for almost a decade to well over a thousand undergraduate students, seminary students, and research doctoral students. More than a few have informed me that they are not really that "in" to history. A few have even nodded off in class—doubtless a reflection of their lack of sleep rather than my abilities as a teacher! Truth told, I can remember a season in my life when history seemed less than appealing, though that changed my junior year of high school in an advanced placement United States history course taught by Coach Joe Haluski. At best, many people have a utilitarian view of history; they care to the degree they find history useful for the stuff that *really* matters in life. Almost everyone can quote at least a paraphrase of George Santayana's famous quip, "Those who cannot remember the past are condemned to repeat it."[3]

The purpose of this book is to provide an introduction to the discipline of history from the perspective of a Christian worldview that is shaped by the great tradition and is in dialog with other key voices in the field. In keeping with the purpose of the Reclaiming the Christian Intellectual Tradition series, I am writing primarily for an undergraduate audience, especially those who wish to major or minor in a field such as history or history education. However, I hope this book will also prove useful to graduate students, college professors, teachers, home educators, public historians, and even armchair historians—anyone who is interested in the study of the past. It is not intended as a comprehensive introduction to history. There are many

---

[2] C. S. Lewis, "On the Reading of Old Books," in *God in the Dock: Essays on Theology and Ethics* (Grand Rapids, MI: Eerdmans, 1972), 200. This essay was originally published in 1944 as Lewis's introduction to a new edition of Athanasius's *The Incarnation of the Word of God*.
[3] George Santayana, *The Life of Reason: Or the Phases of Human Progress* (New York: Charles Scribner's Sons, 1920), 284. Many people claim that Santayana himself was paraphrasing the famous Irish politician and orator Edmund Burke (1729–1797), but I have not found this quote in Burke's writings.

important topics I discuss only in passing or even pass over completely such as historical fallacies and questions of causation, contingency, or counterfactuals.[4] This book will be most useful if it is read as a companion volume to a standard introductory historical textbook that covers these topics and others in a more substantial manner.[5]

HISTORY AND CHRISTIANITY

History is important for several reasons. History is normally considered one of the core disciplines in a modern education. Furthermore, history is foundational to the other disciplines one might choose to study. Every discipline arose at a particular point in time, developed in particular contexts, and possesses a history unto itself. Any good English teacher, ethicist, philosopher, political scientist, musician, doctor, lawyer, pastor, or businessperson has some awareness of the history of his or her vocation. Students who aspire to become historians need to understand foundational issues such as the nature of history, different approaches to history, and the various ways the study of history benefits historians and others. Christian students in particular also need to understand how to address these topics from the perspective of a Christian worldview and how to engage the controversial issue of the relationship between one's faith and the study of history.

Christians should be keenly interested in studying the past since the very truth of the Judeo-Christian tradition is dependent upon certain historical events. Some religious traditions are ahistorical; whether the events referenced in their sacred writings really happened has no effect on the religion. This is not true for the Christian religion, which is at its root a historical faith. Christianity is

---

[4] For helpful introductions to these topics, see Eileen Ka-May Cheng, *Historiography: An Introductory Guide* (London and New York: Bloomsbury Academic, 2012); David Hackett Fischer, *Historians' Fallacies: Toward a Logic of Historical Thought* (New York: Harper and Row, 1970); John Lewis Gaddis, *The Landscape of History: How Historians Map the Past* (New York: Oxford University Press, 2002), 91–110.

[5] I would recommend Gaddis, *Landscape of History*; and James M. Banner Jr., *Being a Historian: An Introduction to the Professional World of History* (New York: Cambridge University Press, 2012).

grounded in events that Christians believe were real, historical occurrences. For example, we believe that at particular points in history Abraham migrated from Ur to Palestine; Moses led the Israelites out of Egyptian slavery; David became the king of Israel; Isaiah and Jeremiah served as prophets; Jesus of Nazareth preached and was crucified; and Paul established churches all over the Roman Empire. Furthermore, Christians believe that the miracles described in the Scriptures are just as valid historically as the more mundane events recorded. In fact, the most important events in Scripture are the miraculous, especially the incarnation of Jesus Christ and his bodily resurrection from the dead. When Christians recite the Apostles' Creed, they confess that Jesus "suffered under Pontius Pilate, was crucified, dead, and buried. He descended into hell. On the third day he rose again from the dead."[6] The truthfulness of Christianity depends upon the historical validity of the events recorded in the Bible.

Christianity is a historical faith. Yet, the Bible is much more than simply a historically rooted—and historically accurate—book. The Bible also provides Christians with a particular worldview that affects every aspect of our lives. According to Philip Ryken,

> A worldview—or "world-and-life view," as some people call it—is the structure of understanding that we use to make sense of our world. Our worldview is what we presuppose. It is our way of looking at life, our interpretation of the universe, our orientation to reality.[7]

As Albert Wolters rightly suggests, "everyone has a worldview, however inarticulate he or she may be in expressing it."[8] Your worldview provides the framework for how you answer life's ultimate

---

[6] Contrary to legend, the twelve apostles did not write the Apostles' Creed; the document dates to the fourth century. Most versions of the creed suggest Jesus descended into hell, but because Christians debate precisely what that language means, some traditions omit it from the creed.

[7] Philip Graham Ryken, *Christian Worldview: A Student's Guide*, Reclaiming the Christian Intellectual Tradition (Wheaton, IL: Crossway, 2013), 19.

[8] Albert M. Wolters, *Creation Regained: Biblical Basics for a Reformational Worldview*, 2nd ed. (Grand Rapids, MI: Eerdmans, 2005), 4.

questions. Where did humanity come from? What is the meaning of life? Is there a God or gods who are in control of this world? Is there such a thing as right and wrong? Does life continue after death? Is knowledge even possible? As your worldview helps you answer these questions, it in turn influences everything about you, including all of your actions, attitudes, and priorities.

The Christian worldview is rooted in the story of God's creation, humanity's fall into sin, and the redemption accomplished through the life, death, and resurrection of Jesus Christ—what has been aptly called the true story of the whole world.[9] It helps us to think rightly about God and live rightly before him. It gives shape to our worship, witness, and ethics. It provides the proper grid through which we should interpret all of life—including history. In chapter 3, we will elaborate on the Christian worldview and discuss some specific ways that it ought to inform a Christian approach to history.

THE GREAT COMMANDMENTS AND THE CHRISTIAN HISTORIAN

Within the broader story that makes up the Christian worldview, we find many motivations, priorities, and ethics that arise from the biblical narrative. Along those lines, the two "great commandments" represent a key biblical theme with particular importance for Christian historians. In Matthew 22:34–39, a lawyer asks Jesus's opinion about the greatest commandment in God's law. Jesus responds by giving two commandments that are closely related to each other. The greatest commandment is to love the Lord with all your heart, soul, and mind. The second is to love your neighbor as yourself. When all is said and done, the most important difference between a Christian historian and a non-Christian historian is primarily a matter of motivation. The great commandments speak directly to this point.

---

[9] See Michael W. Goheen and Craig G. Bartholomew, *Living at the Crossroads: An Introduction to Christian Worldview* (Grand Rapids, MI: Baker Academic, 2008), 1–10.

For the believing historian, historical inquiry—as with every other aspect of life—is ultimately an act of worship done for the Lord. Paul writes, "So, whether you eat or drink, or whatever you do, do all to the glory of God" (1 Cor. 10:31). This includes the study of history, which should always be to the Lord and for his glory, whether the subject is the history of Scotch Presbyterian immigrants in the Appalachian mountains or the history of agriculture in medieval Europe. Quality research that conforms to the highest standards in the historical profession brings glory to the God who alone is perfect and who is reflected in our own imperfect attempts at excellence.

The second great commandment, also known as the Golden Rule, is especially relevant to the way we study the past. Christian historians are called to practice neighbor-love toward their subjects by empathizing with them. This means the believing historian is called to truly understand and appreciate why people in the past did what they did, even when the historian disagrees with the action itself. Christian historians also seek to interpret past events as honestly and charitably as is possible. This is sometimes very difficult. What historian wants to be charitable to pirates who raped and pillaged British sailors or to Nazi soldiers who gassed Jews at Auschwitz? The past can be an ugly place. Nevertheless, believing historians will do their very best to interpret the past in the same way they would want future historians to interpret them in the present—honestly and charitably, disagreements notwithstanding. As Beth Barton Schweiger argues, we must love the subjects of our history, even when we disagree with them, if we are to accurately understand them.[10] Rightly remembering the past is a spiritual discipline for Christian historians (and all believers).[11]

The Golden Rule also affects the way Christian historians ap-

---

[10] Beth Barton Schweiger, "Seeing Things: Knowledge and Love in History," in *Confessing History: Explorations in Christian Faith and the Historian's Vocation*, eds. John Fea, Jay Green, and Eric Miller (Notre Dame, IN: University of Notre Dame Press, 2010), 61.

[11] For more on this theme, see Miroslav Volf, *The End of Memory: Remembering Rightly in a Violent World* (Grand Rapids, MI: Eerdmans, 2006); and Margaret Bendroth, *The Spiritual Practice of Remembering* (Grand Rapids, MI: Eerdmans, 2013).

proach their sources. In 2002, two of the best-selling popular historians in America, Stephen Ambrose and Doris Kearns Goodwin, were charged with plagiarism.[12] There is hardly a more serious offense for a researcher, especially a historian. The Writing Tutorial Services at Indiana University offers an excellent, simple definition of plagiarism: "Plagiarism is using others' ideas and words without clearly acknowledging the source of that information."[13] For the Christian, plagiarism is not only a matter of stealing from another—a practice certainly incompatible with a Christian ethic (Ex. 20:15)—but it is also a clear violation of neighbor-love. When you cite the work of another historian without giving credit for his or her ideas, you are not treating the other historian as you would wish to be treated if you were in his or her place. When interacting with the writings of others, the Christian historian gives "honor to whom honor is owed" (Rom. 13:7).

The Christian worldview impacts the study of history in many ways. Unfortunately, many historians never give so much as a passing thought to the relationship between their discipline and the Christian faith. Fortunately, there is good news: even historians who are not Christians have been influenced by the Christian worldview in more ways than they realize. John Sommerville notes six different "vestiges of Christian scholarship" that can be found among most professional historians in the West: (1) a sense of human sinfulness; (2) a linear view of history; (3) a focus on history as a story with a beginning, middle, and end; (4) skepticism of the idea of progress; (5) belief in human freedom; and (6) an ironic approach to historiography.[14] I will tease out many of these ideas in the coming chapters. As Jim Patterson suggests in his own discus-

---

[12] Fred Barnes, "Stephen Ambrose, Copycat," *The Weekly Standard*, June 14, 2002, accessed May 14, 2014, http://www.weeklystandard.com/Content/Public/Articles/000/000/000/738lfddv.asp; Bo Crader, "A Historian and Her Sources," *The Weekly Standard*, January 28, 2002, accessed May 14, 2014, http://www.weeklystandard.com/Content/Public/Articles/000/000/000/793ihurw.asp.
[13] "Plagiarism: What It Is and How to Recognize and Avoid It," Writing Tutorial Services, Indiana University, accessed May 14, 2014, http://www.indiana.edu/~wts/pamphlets/plagiarism.shtml.
[14] C. John Sommerville, "Christian Historiography? A Pragmatic Approach," *Fides et Historia*, Winter/Spring 2003: 2–3.

sion of Sommerville's list, "Christians who study, teach, or write history should be encouraged by these signals of common grace."[15] I agree. In many ways, the Christian historian openly owns certain truths that many nonbelieving historians seem to know only by intuition. Unlike the non-Christian historian, the believing historian is able to give praise to the One who has provided these intellectual tools to those who study the past.

WHAT LIES AHEAD

Now that we have addressed some important preliminary considerations, we are ready to dive deeper into the discipline of history. Chapter 1 will answer the question, "What is history?" by making a key distinction between the past and history. It will also introduce the basics of historical research and identify several different types of history. Chapter 2 will discuss different schools of historical interpretation and critique them from the perspective of the Christian worldview. The chapter will also briefly introduce the topic of historiography. Chapter 3 will focus upon the oft-debated relationship between faith and history. How do various Christian historians interpret the past? How does the doctrine of providence relate to historical interpretation? This chapter, more than any other, will examine some of the challenges uniquely faced by Christian historians. Chapter 4 extends an invitation to the discipline of history. It will discuss some of the various vocations for which formal historical training can help prepare a student. It will also suggest ways that history can be brought to bear in other disciplines and vocations.

---

[15] James A. Patterson, "The Study of History," in *Faith and Learning: A Handbook for Christian Higher Education*, ed. David S. Dockery (Nashville: B&H Academic, 2012), 235.

✚ 1

UNDERSTANDING HISTORY

A historian, then, characteristically argues, presenting reasons for adopting a particular version of the past. He is trying to persuade his reader to adopt his own view.[1]

David Bebbington

One evening, my wife, Leah, and I were enjoying dinner with our friends Keith and Amy. After dinner, Amy referenced how a recent biographical movie misrepresented its subject. She conceded that the film included the disclaimer that it is "based on a true story" rather than a perfectly accurate recounting of the events it depicts. Nevertheless, Amy complained that the movie is grossly inaccurate and suggested that filmmakers should not rewrite history. Of course, I knew exactly what she meant. Who among us has not been frustrated when a film that claims to be historically accurate takes any number of (ahem) "liberties" for the sake of artistry? But, since I was feeling a bit spunky that night, I suggested to Amy that historians rewrite history all the time. What followed was a lively discussion about the relationship between history and the past. Keith, who literally called while I was writing this paragraph, jokes that he and Amy are still having trouble trusting any historians after that conversation. I am not sure if I am an exception to their distrust or not!

---

[1] David Bebbington, *Patterns in History: A Christian Perspective on Historical Thought* (Nottingham, UK: Inter-Varsity, 1979; repr., Vancouver, British Columbia: Regent College Publishing, 1990), 14.

HISTORY IS NOT THE PAST

In my experience, most people believe that the words "history" and "the past" are more or less the same thing. In some respects, this is only natural; in everyday language, these two terms are used as synonyms. If you asked the proverbial "man on the street" to define the word *history*, he would probably say something like "history is what happened in the past." If this is indeed how we ought to understand history, then it only makes sense that the purpose of the historian is to tell us about what happened in the past, to remind us of the who, when, what, where, and why of bygone days. While there is a legitimate place for such chronicling of the past, to equate the historian with the chronicler introduces a category error that has important consequences for the discipline of history.

Professional historians make a distinction between the past and history. The past includes events that occurred prior to this particular moment in time. It might be many centuries before right now, or it might be yesterday. The past is vast. To be sure, it is possible to relate important aspects of the past to present-day audiences. For example, I can tell my students with relative certainty that Marcus Aurelius ruled the Roman Empire as coemperor or sole emperor from AD 161 to 180. However, there are innumerable things about Marcus Aurelius that even the most prodigious historian will never know. Because no one except God was around in the past, he alone has a complete understanding of it. Many history teachers focus almost exclusively on rehearsing the past, forcing students to learn about names, dates, and key events. Lazy engagement with the past is the reason many students do not care much for history; they have never been properly introduced.

For the historian, history is not the same thing as the past, but rather, history is the discipline of reconstructing and interpreting the past. Historians believe that history includes more than simply repeating facts about the past. John Lewis Gaddis suggests that the past is something we can never have exactly as it was when it happened. He claims, "We cannot relive, retrieve, or rerun it as we might some laboratory experiment or computer simulation." Gaddis suggests that, at best, we can only "represent" the past.[2] This is the unique task of the historian, and it is a task that necessarily involves interpretation because of our distance from the past events themselves.

History has always involved interpretation, even before the birth of the modern academic discipline of history in the nineteenth century. Tacitus (c. AD 56–117), the famous senator and historian of the Roman Empire, wrote during a period of decline. He offered a declension narrative, a story of falling away from an earlier ideal, which moralized against the ethical and political corruptions that he believed led to Rome's decline. In a completely different vein, Eusebius of Caesarea (c. AD 260–340), the most important early historian of Christianity, offered a triumphalistic interpretation where all of human history culminated in the conversion of Constantine and his consolidation of imperial power in the Roman Empire. Historical objectivity has always been an elusive goal for the historian, though many professional historians have tried hard to chase after that impossible dream.[3]

It is fairly common to hear people complain about "revisionist" historians who are reinventing the past. Historical revisionism is the reinterpretation of received, popular, or prominent understandings of history; others can view revisionism either positively or negatively. In contemporary America, complaints about historical revisionism frequently seem to be motivated by political concerns. For example, many of those on the political right believe that theologically conservative evangelicals played a central role in America's founding.[4]

---

[2] John Lewis Gaddis, *The Landscape of History: How Historians Map the Past* (New York: Oxford University Press, 2002), 3.

[3] For an influential study of this topic, see Peter Novick, *That Noble Dream: The "Objectivity Question" and the American Historical Profession* (New York: Cambridge University Press, 1998).

[4] For two thoughtful recent books that engage with this widely held view, see John Fea, *Was America Founded as a Christian Nation?* (Louisville, KY: Westminster-John Knox, 2011); and John D. Wilsey, *One Nation Under God? An Evangelical Critique of Christian America* (Eugene, OR: Pickwick, 2011).

For these folks, the most vocal of whom are often more interested in activism than history, America was intended to be a Christian nation. Any deviation from our Christian heritage is a sign of declension. By contrast, for many on the political left, America is a nation of oppressors where those with the power suppressed the rights of minorities, immigrants, the poor, women, and homosexuals. For these folks, again, often concerned mostly with activism, America is moving in the right direction, especially since the 1960s.[5] Most historians agree that these two popular understandings of the past fail to accurately reconstruct American history.

The past can be a powerful tool in advancing a contemporary agenda. Those with a vested interest in preserving a particular understanding of the past are sometimes distraught when a historian upsets the apple cart by challenging their interpretation. William Katerberg suggests these tensions "often seem to come down to a battle between academic history and public memory."[6] Sweeping complaints about historical revisionism misunderstand the nature of history. As John Fea rightly argues, all historians are revisionists because all historians are doing their best to interpret some aspect of the past with the best source material available to them.[7] The problem is not with historical revisionism per se, but with revisionism that is clearly driven by a *presentist* agenda and/or that claims to offer the definitive interpretation of the past. (I discuss the dangers of presentism in the next section.) Any good historian understands that history is always a provisional discipline. Christian historians might add that we see through a glass darkly (1 Cor. 13:12) and that the secret things belong to God alone (Deut. 29:29). As new evidence comes to light, new interpretations will arise that

---

[5] The best-known book from this perspective is Howard Zinn, *A People's History of the United States: 1492 to Present* (New York: Harper Perennial Modern Classics, 2005).

[6] William Katerberg, "The 'Objectivity Question' and the Historian's Vocation," in *Confessing History: Explorations in Christian Faith and the Historian's Vocation*, eds. John Fea, Jay Green, and Eric Miller (Notre Dame, IN: University of Notre Dame Press, 2010), 109.

[7] John Fea, *Why Study History? Reflecting on the Importance of the Past* (Grand Rapids, MI: Baker Academic, 2013), 15.

complement, challenge, and, at times, correct older interpretations. The past may have already passed, but history will always be a work in progress.

A LONG TIME AGO, IN A GALAXY FAR, FAR AWAY . . .

Ever since the original *Star Wars* movie opened in theaters in 1977, the words mentioned above have been a part of American popular culture. Each of the live-action movies in the *Star Wars* franchise that have been released thus far begin with these words set against a black screen. Cue the famous theme song by composer John Williams. Once the music begins, a short summary of the backstory leading up to the film scrolls upward across the screen. Once the prologue is completed, the movie begins. I get chill bumps every time I sit in a theater and the opening words appear on the screen; even my disappointment in the moribund second trilogy of movies could not take away this feeling of anticipation. With a new trilogy of *Star Wars* films set to be released beginning in 2015, I hope each movie begins in the same way. (Are you listening, Disney?)

In a helpful article on historical thinking, Thomas Andrews and Flannery Burke suggest that the opening sequence in the *Star Wars* films reminds us of the importance of historical context.[8] I believe it also offers another important reminder to historians. The past, while often open to scholarly study, took place a long time ago in a faraway place (if not another galaxy). Many historians emphasize this point by citing the famous opening line to L. P. Hartley's 1953 novel *The Go-Between*: "The past is a foreign country; they do things differently there."[9] This is true even of the recent past. For this reason, historians must take into account matters

---

[8] Thomas Andrews and Flannery Burke, "What Does It Mean to Think Historically?" *Perspectives on History*, January 2007, accessed October 3, 2014, http://www.historians.org/publications-and-directories/perspectives-on-history/january-2007/what-does-it-mean-to-think-historically.

[9] Most famously, see David Lowenthal, *The Past is a Foreign Country* (Cambridge and New York: Cambridge University Press, 1985), which is primarily a critique of nonprofessional misuses and abuses of the past. For other historians who play off of this language, see Fea, *Why Study History?* 47–63; and Carl R. Trueman, *Histories and Fallacies: Problems Faced in the Writing of History* (Wheaton, IL: Crossway, 2010), 109–40.

of historical context when studying the past. You might think of historical context as everything that was in the atmosphere at the time of the subject you are studying. According to one introductory textbook, historical context "might be seen as the setting of the period" and includes "the social, cultural, political, economic, and technological milieu of the day."[10] Christian historians (really, any good historian) would point out historical context also includes the religious and other worldview assumptions from the period under consideration.

A keen sense of historical context helps protect historians from the temptation of presentism, which is any attempt to read present assumptions back into the past. Professional historians work hard to avoid presentism. As Gordon Wood notes,

> The present should not be the criterion for what we find in the past. Our perceptions and explanations of the past should not be directly shaped by the issues and problems of our own time. The best and most serious historians have come to know that, even when their original impulse to write history came from a pressing present problem. . . .
>
> The more we study the events and situations in the past, the more complicated and complex we find them to be. The impulse of the best historians is always to penetrate ever more deeply into the circumstances of the past and to explain the complicated context of past events. The past in the hands of expert historians becomes a different world, a complicated world that requires considerable historical imagination to recover with any degree of accuracy.[11]

Presentism lends itself to a number of common historical fallacies. According to David Hackett Fischer, "A fallacy is not merely an error itself, but a way of falling into error. It consists in [sic] false

---

[10] Michael J. Galgano, J. Chris Arndt, and Raymond M. Hyser, *Doing History: Research and Writing in the Digital Age* (Belmont, CA: Wadsworth Cengage, 2008), 4.

[11] Gordon S. Wood, *The Purpose of the Past: Reflections on the Uses of History* (New York: Penguin, 2008), 10.

reasoning, often from true factual premises, so that false conclusions are generated."[12] Historical fallacies are rife within popular accounts of the past and can even be found among incautious professional historians.

Casual students of history frequently assume that what is true of the present was true of the past in more or less equivalent ways. For example, consider the history of the civil rights movement. Observers sometimes assume that civil rights activists in the 1950s and 1960s were theological liberals because they were also political liberals. After all, it is quite common today, in America at least, to closely associate liberal politics and liberal theology with one another (the same holds true for conservative politics and conservative theology). Nevertheless, as David Chappell has demonstrated, while civil rights activists were all over the map theologically, many held fairly orthodox views of human sinfulness and the need for personal redemption through faith in Jesus Christ.[13] It would be incorrect to simplistically assume that what is true of the present—or at least seems to be true—was true of the past in exactly the same way. This is not to suggest that no continuity exists between the past and present; continuity can be demonstrated in countless ways. Christians assert there is nothing new under the sun (Eccles. 1:9); on one level, this is absolutely true. Christian historians, however, should remember that the sun shines differently, depending upon where one is standing; the shadows are always moving and sometimes clouds obstruct our view of the sky.

A particularly common version of presentism bears mention: the oft-cited "whig" interpretation of history. In 1931, the Eng-

---

[12] Fischer has catalogued the most common of these fallacies in his classic work on the subject. See David Hackett Fischer, *Historians' Fallacies: Toward a Logic of Historical Thought* (New York: Harper and Row, 1970). More recently, Carl Trueman has discussed how historians are often not careful enough when studying the history of ideas in particular. See Trueman, *Histories and Fallacies*.

[13] David L. Chappell, *A Stone of Hope: Prophetic Religion and the Death of Jim Crow* (Chapel Hill, NC: University of North Carolina Press, 2004).

lish historian and devout Methodist Herbert Butterfield published *The Whig Interpretation of History*. Butterfield suggested that many modern historians were overly "Protestant, progressive, and whig" in their understanding of history.[14] The latter is a reference to the British political tradition that emphasized the inevitability of greater liberty, democracy, and enlightenment. For Butterfield, the problem with the whig interpretation of history is "that it studies the past with reference to the present."[15] In other words, it is a form of presentism. However, what sets the whig interpretation apart is its assumption that the past is prologue to the present and that the present is more progressive, enlightened, and, well, *better* than the past. Thus, the past is often judged by the degree to which it measures up to the standards of the present. While Butterfield was interested primarily in British political history, the whig interpretation has become a common label used to describe any overly progressive form of presentism, regardless of the subject under consideration.

Remembering our distance from the past helps to keep careful historians humble. This should be especially important to Christian historians, for whom humility is both a professional best practice and a spiritual virtue. Every historian studies the past from a particular point of view. In the case of a believing historian, the Christian worldview will be integral to that perspective. Nevertheless, the past deserves to be understood according to its own terms, insofar as this is possible. While there might be any number of legitimate ways to apply insights from the past to the present, the past deserves to be treated as more than the preamble to the present. The discipline of history recognizes that the study of the past is a worthwhile end in itself, even when the subject being studied has little to no bearing on the present. If God created everything that is, and if he providentially rules all things according to his

---

[14] Herbert Butterfield, *The Whig Interpretation of History* (New York: Charles Scribner's Sons, 1931), 3.
[15] Ibid., 11.

sovereign purposes, then every moment in the past matters to God. The past should also matter to historians enough to be treated with the respect it deserves.

THE TOOLS OF THE TRADE

Every discipline is characterized in part by the tools of its trade. From 1947 until they sold the business in 2012, my grandparents and then parents owned a company that focused on brake repair for automobiles and general parts and service for semitrailer trucks. Both my father and grandfather are natural-born mechanics. For over six decades, they surrounded themselves with men who were gifted mechanics—some of them even more so than Dad and Granddaddy. From the time I was a little boy, I was out in the shop "helping" the mechanics. The tools they used in their trade always fascinated me: hydraulic vehicle lifts, impact wrenches, several different types of grease, large rubber mallets, to name only a few. Incidentally, despite my family heritage, by the time I was a teenager it was clear to all interested parties that the Lord skipped me when he was handing out the more mechanical gifts. For many years, I worked part-time during the school year and full-time during the summers for the family business. I sold parts, shelved inventory, and drove a delivery truck. Everyone kept me as far away from the tools as possible.

As in all disciplines, historians use certain tools of the trade in interpreting the past. These tools can be divided into two categories: primary sources and secondary sources. Primary sources are firsthand materials that come directly from a past individual or institution from the period being studied. These artifacts are the most important tools in reconstructing the past because they represent our direct connection with the subject under consideration. Many primary sources are written artifacts such as letters, journals, books, articles, reports, and records. Others are material artifacts such as property and possessions. Any artifact produced during the period being studied is a potential primary source. Primary sources are our windows to the past.

For example, consider the historian who is writing a doctoral dissertation on Martin Luther King Jr. Obviously, she would want to look at every primary source she can that is directly related to King. Relevant sources would include his journals, correspondence, sermon manuscripts, audiovisual recordings of his speeches, published essays, unpublished manuscripts, personal Bible, and perhaps the suit King was wearing the day he was assassinated. At the same time, our historian would also want to look at other primary sources from the same period that will help her to understand King's historical context. She would want to study sources such as civil rights legislation, newspaper editorials, speeches by public officials, government memos, correspondence about King, television news reports, eulogies of King after his death, and oral interviews with those who knew him. The more primary source material the historian engages, the greater the potential to accurately understand King's world.

In some cases, primary sources have been published and are widely accessible. For example, in the case of Martin Luther King Jr., one publisher has produced an anthology including his most important speeches and essays.[16] Another publisher has published six volumes thus far in a multivolume critical edition of King's personal papers.[17] Increasingly, unpublished primary source material is being scanned or transcribed and made available online by libraries and archives. For example, the King Center Library and Archives in Atlanta, Georgia, and Martin Luther King, Jr. Research and Education Institute at Stanford University have made some of King's primary source material available at their respective websites.[18] As

---

[16] James M. Washington, ed., *A Testament of Hope: The Essential Writings and Speeches of Martin Luther King, Jr.* (New York: HarperOne, 2003).

[17] Martin Luther King Jr., *The Papers of Martin Luther King, Jr.*, ed. Clayborne Carson, 6 vols. (Berkeley, CA: University of California Press, 1992–2007).

[18] See the King Center Library and Archives (http://www.thekingcenter.org/king-library-archive) and the Martin Luther King, Jr. Research and Education Institute at Stanford University (http://king institute.stanford.edu/king-papers/about-papers-project).

a general rule, historians need to use online primary sources only when they are available on a credible scholarly website. For student researchers, your professors can help you discern which websites are appropriate and which are not.

Most primary source material in this world remains unpublished and is housed in archival collections, libraries, museums, and sometimes even personal families or private foundations. This is especially the case with artifacts such as personal journals, correspondence, internal memos, etc. For the historian researching King, archival research would need to be conducted in the aforementioned archives in Atlanta and Stanford as well as in archival collections at Morehouse College in Atlanta and the Library of Congress in Washington, DC. In addition, the historian would need to work with many other archival collections that might include correspondence from King to other individuals whose papers are housed there. Unless you are studying a topic where all of the primary source material is published and/or accessible via appropriate websites, it is normally necessary to spend at least some time digging around in archival collections as you conduct your research.

Secondary sources represent another of the historian's key tools of the trade. Secondary sources are the works of other scholars who have studied your subject. Secondary sources include essays in scholarly books, unpublished papers delivered at a historical conference or similar setting, biographies, entries in encyclopedias and dictionaries, dissertations, monographs, and scholarly journal articles. Searching relevant databases such as WorldCat, EBSCO, and ATLA will help you to learn about the secondary sources that have been published on your topic. As a general rule, historians try to avoid popular biographies, applicatory or self-help books ("leadership lessons from" or "the wit and wisdom of"), textbooks, and narrative historical surveys. In the case of encyclopedias and dictionaries, historians try to stick to those publications closest to their topic. For example, an entry about Martin Luther King Jr. in *Encyclopedia Britannica* is too general to be useful, but an entry from *The Martin Luther King, Jr., Encyclopedia* might be very helpful.[19]

Monographs and scholarly journal articles are normally the most important secondary sources because they are refereed or peer-reviewed. This means the scholarly community has vetted these works and agreed that they make a scholarly contribution to the existing body of knowledge about the subject. A monograph is a book-length essay that studies a specialized topic. Rather than providing an introductory or summary treatment to a broad subject, like a textbook or a general biography, a monograph defends a thesis related to a topic. For example, while dozens of historians (and journalists) have written biographies of Martin Luther King Jr. or general histories of the civil rights movement, Thomas Jackson has recently published a monograph arguing that King's agenda broadened beyond desegregation and voting rights after the early 1960s to focus more upon other human rights, especially economic justice.[20]

Like monographs, scholarly journal articles advance a thesis on a specialized topic related to their subject. The best journal articles are published in periodicals that are peer-reviewed. While helpful scholarly essays are sometimes published in journals where articles are not subjected to peer review, as a general rule historians try to stick with refereed journals because those articles have been read by other scholars and revised based upon feedback prior to publication. For example, suppose a historian writes an essay on Martin Luther King Jr.'s use of the book of Exodus in his speeches about racial desegregation. If he published that article in a popular

[19] Clayborne Carson et al., eds., *The Martin Luther King, Jr., Encyclopedia* (Westport, CT: Greenwood, 2008).

[20] Thomas F. Jackson, *From Civil Rights to Human Rights: Martin Luther King, Jr., and the Struggle for Economic Justice*, Politics and Culture in Modern America (Philadelphia: University of Pennsylvania Press, 2007).

preaching journal, it is possible that many readers, including some historians, might find it insightful. However, other scholars have likely not scrutinized it. Conversely, an article on the same topic published in a refereed journal such as the *Journal of American History*, *Church History*, the *Journal of Southern History*, or the *Journal of Southern Religion* has been put through the scholarly wringer and judged to be a worthwhile contribution to our scholarly understanding of King, his preaching, and the rhetoric of the civil rights movement.

Good historians learn which tools they need for their discipline, where to find them, and how to use them. Christian historians should be especially concerned with excellence in historical research and interpretation. Believing historians should want to find the very best primary and secondary sources so that they can thoroughly understand their subject in its original historical context. God is glorified in the pursuit of scholarly excellence, and in the discipline of history; this means the hard work of comprehensive, careful research. The principle of neighbor-love, referenced in the introduction, should further inspire the Christian historian to be especially scrupulous in using these sources in such a way that empathizes with the subject and represents it as accurately as possible.

TYPES OF HISTORY

If you have visited a bookstore like Barnes and Noble, you may have browsed through the "History" or "Biography" sections. You perhaps noticed some individual authors who have written on a wide variety of historical topics from many places stretching across vast expanses of time. Many of these authors are journalists. Some are trained historians. The books they write might be informative, well written, and may even be recognized with a Pulitzer Prize. Some of my favorite books fall into this category, although, generally speaking, they are works of popular history rather than professional history. As such, while perhaps a joy to read, these books often lack the nuance and scholarly rigor that characterizes the writings of most professional historians. The reason is that trained historians are specialists who have focused on a particular aspect of history and become experts in that field. They have a good knowledge of history in general, but the closer they get to their expertise, the greater the depth of their historical understanding. For the Christian historian, cultivating this sort of academic expertise is a matter of glorifying God through the pursuit of excellence.

History is divided into many different fields of expertise, and nearly every professional historian has specialized training in one or sometimes two of these fields. For example, diplomatic historians, military historians, economic historians, religious historians, gender historians, and environmental historians study people, themes, and events from the past related to these broader topics. Sometimes these fields closely overlap with other disciplines. For example, some diplomatic historians might work in a university department that focuses upon political science or political theory. Some religious historians, on the other hand, might work in a religion department or at a seminary or divinity school. Gender historians are as likely to be in a women's studies department as a history department. Most historians further narrow their field by geography and period. For example, a military historian might be an expert on the Vietnam War, a diplomatic historian might be an expert on Russian and Japanese relations prior to the Russo-Japanese War, and a religious historian might focus on Islam in North Africa in the ninth century.

Until relatively recently, historians have tended to focus upon those individuals that might be considered the most significant past figures. In most cases, these men (they were normally men) were educated people who represented the ethnic majority and economic, political, and educational elite of their particular context.

In part, this is because subjects who fit this profile left most of the available primary source material. Many historians were either biographers who focused upon individuals or intellectual historians who focused upon ideas. Even historians who devoted their study to broader topics or extended periods of time tended to focus on key individuals and their thought. However, in recent decades, professional historians have increasingly focused upon subjects that do not fit this paradigm. As a result, biography and intellectual history are less popular among historians than was once the case, though the latter has been making a comeback in recent years.[21] Furthermore, diplomatic history in particular, which of necessity focuses upon cultural elites, is far less prominent than it was in earlier decades.

This change has been occasioned by the growing popularity of two types of history that originated in continental Europe before becoming popular with North American scholars. Since the 1960s, many historians have focused their attention more upon ordinary people rather than cultural elites. Originally called the "new social history," scholars in this school of thought have incorporated social sciences such as sociology and statistical research into the discipline of history and have helped launch several new subfields within the discipline such as ethnic history, gender history, urban history, labor history, and family history.[22] Ethnic minorities, women, children, immigrants, and the poor receive far more treatment from historians than was once the case. In addition to birthing new fields, social historians have influenced older fields. Many military historians now focus upon common soldiers and civilian populations rather than officers, strategies, and key battles. Many religious historians focus upon women, minorities, individual

---

[21] For example, the Society for US Intellectual History was organized in 2007 because of renewed interest in the field. See the S-USIH website at http://s-usih.org/ (accessed October 3, 2014).

[22] For an interpretive essay of the new social history and its early influence among professional historians, see Laurence Veysey, "The 'New' Social History in the Context of American Historical Writing," *Reviews in American History* 7, no.1 (March 1979): 1–12.

believers, and adherents of alternative religions rather than leading clergy, doctrines, controversies, and major world religions.

Since the mid-1970s, some historians have opted for cultural history rather than social history.[23] Cultural historians incorporate anthropology into their research and focus their attention on the customs, arts, manners, and habits of groups of people. Cultural historians study such topics as popular culture, the media, public perceptions of a given subject, and concepts such as power, class, and race. As with social history, cultural history has affected older fields of study. Political historians might study how a concept such as "liberty" or "big government" or "monarchy" is perceived by different groups of people in a given culture. Religious historians might consider how Jesus or Mohammed has been interpreted in popular culture or why some people groups are friendlier toward converting to a new religion than others. Like social history, cultural history also fits well with interdisciplinary settings in colleges and universities such as an American studies department, an African American studies department, or a religion department.

Social history and cultural history are now the most popular fields within the discipline. They arose during a cultural context in the 1960s and 1970s when a generation of rising scholars was less inclined toward patriotism, traditional religion, and Judeo-Christian morality. These tendencies were shaped by sometimes-overlapping cultural trends such as feminism, the youth counterculture, the sexual revolution, the civil rights movement, mistrust of government due to the Vietnam War and the Watergate scandal, and increased immigration from Asia and Africa. For historians who came of age during the Baby Boomer generation, studying the lives and ideas of "dead white men" seemed regressive, even insidious, because it potentially reinforced the narratives of those who held cultural power and contributed to the marginalization of women, ethnic

---

[23] See Lynn Hunt, ed., *The New Cultural History*, Studies on the History of Society and Culture (Berkeley and Los Angeles: University of California Press, 1989).

minorities, the poor, immigrants, and those who embraced moralities outside the majority. Social and cultural history came to dominate entire history departments at many universities, though some historians have criticized this trend.[24]

What should a Christian who wants to be a historian think about these various types of history? In principle, Christians should be open to any and all approaches to history, even those that began among people who sometimes embraced a non- or even anti-Christian worldview. Social historians are studying subjects that were ignored by earlier generations. Christian social historians have the opportunity to show neighbor-love to the poor, oppressed, marginalized, or just plain ignored by incorporating their stories into more culturally dominant or popular historical narratives. Christian cultural historians have a similar opportunity to complement traditional interpretations of the past by recovering and interpreting untold stories and offering new angles on well-known subjects. Many Christians, especially in the Reformed tradition, have argued since at least the time of Augustine that "all truth is God's truth."[25] When applied to the discipline of history, we might say that heretofore obscure subjects are worthy of studying, and doing so in new and creative ways, because everything matters to God.

A key difference between Christian and some non-Christian historians is that the Christian historian understands that less-fashionable approaches to history are also worthy of consideration. Biography, intellectual history, national narratives,

---

[24] See Keith Windschuttle, *The Killing of History: How Literary Critics and Social Theorists are Murdering Our Past* (San Francisco, CA: Encounter, 2000). For a critical, but more measured assessment of social history in particular, see Gertrude Himmelfarb, *The New History and the Old: Critical Essays and Reappraisals*, rev. ed. (Cambridge, MA: Belknap, 2004).

[25] In *On Christian Doctrine*, Augustine wrote, "Nay, but let every good and true Christian understand that wherever truth may be found, it belongs to his Master; and while he recognizes and acknowledges the truth, even in their religious literature, let him reject the figments of superstition." See Augustine, *On Christian Doctrine*, 2:18:28, http://www.ccel.org/ccel/augustine/doctrine.xix_1.html. The slogan "all truth is God's truth" is a paraphrase of Augustine coined in the twentieth century by Frank Gaebelein and then promoted by evangelical thinkers such as Francis Schaeffer and Arthur Holmes. See Albert R. Beck, "All Truth is God's Truth: The Life and Ideas of Frank E. Gaebelein" (PhD diss., Baylor University, 2008).

diplomatic history that focuses on cultural elites, denominational history, and the history of wartime battles are also part of the past and offer an important angle worth studying. Perhaps it is best to say that the Christian historian should be interested in a "thick" understanding of the past that takes into account the best of all the subdisciplines of history and various approaches advocated by scholars. The Christian historian will seek to avoid the extremes of older approaches to history that lack sufficient nuance and ignore those outside the cultural center and newer schools of thought that are at times tempted to elevate peripheral subjects at the expense of those that are more central.

2

HISTORICAL INTERPRETATION

All this being so, we should not ascribe the power of granting kingdoms and empires to any but the true God. It is he who gives happiness in the kingdom of heaven to the godly alone, and it is he who gives earthly kingdoms to the godly and the ungodly alike according to his pleasure, which never takes pleasure in anything unjust. For although we have discussed such things as God willed to make clear to us, it is a task too great for us, and, indeed, it far surpasses our powers to sort out the secrets of the human heart and by clear investigation to weigh up the merits of kingdoms.[1]

Augustine of Hippo

Perhaps you have heard of the old Indian proverb about the blind men and the elephant. According to the story, a group of blind men fall into a pit where an elephant has also been trapped. Each man feels a different part of the elephant. One, feeling the tusk, declares that an elephant is like a spear. Another, feeling the ears, compares an elephant to a fan. Another hugs a leg and concludes that an elephant is like a tree. Still another touches the trunk and claims that the elephant is like a snake. Of course, each blind man is both right and wrong. An elephant is like each of those things—if you only consider one part of the animal's anatomy. But when you take into account the entire elephant, it is like none of those other things. An elephant is like an elephant. I believe

---

[1] Augustine, *The City of God (De Civitate Dei), Books 1–10*, ed. Boniface Ramsey, trans. William Babcock (Hyde Park, NY: New City Press, 2012), 174.

this parable is relevant when it comes to questions of historical interpretation.

In the previous chapter, I argued that history is not the same thing as the past. I discussed historical context and warned against the threat of presentism. I also introduced the tools of the historical trade and introduced you to some of the different types of history. In this chapter, I want to focus upon historical interpretation by introducing you to five different schools of historical thought that have been advanced at various points in the past. I will critique four of them from the perspective of a Christian worldview; the fifth will be the focus of the following chapter. I will then briefly discuss the related topic of historiography, or the history of how historians have interpreted the past.

SCHOOLS OF HISTORY

All historians recognize multiple schools of historical interpretation, though they vary with how they divide and define these schools. In his helpful book *Patterns in History: A Christian Perspective on Historical Thought*, historian David Bebbington offers a Christian introduction to five major schools of historical interpretation: (1) cyclical history; (2) Christian history; (3) the idea of progress; (4) historicism; and (5) Marxist history. In his classic work *The Idea of History*, the philosopher of history R. G. Collingwood divides his discussion into three major schools: (1) Greco-Roman history; (2) Christian history; and (3) scientific history.[2] Historian Jules Benjamin briefly outlines four major schools of thought: (1) the cyclical school; (2) the providentialist school; (3) the progressive school; and (4) the postmodern school.[3] Following Bebbington, I will argue for five schools of thought, each with variations within them: (1) cyclical history; (2) history as progress; (3) historicism; (4) Marxist history; and (5) Judeo-Christian history.

---

[2] R. G. Collingwood, *The Idea of History* (New York: Oxford University Press, 1956).

[3] Jules R. Benjamin, *A Student's Guide to History*, 11th ed. (New York: Bedford/St. Martin's, 2010), 5–6.

CYCLICAL HISTORY

Many Eastern cultures understand history to be cyclical rather than linear.[4] In the cyclical interpretation, history is a series of endlessly repeating cycles. The past is repeated in the present and the present will be repeated in the future. History has no ultimate purpose or goal—it simply happens again and again. History had no starting point and it will have no climax. Each individual cycle of history is irrelevant except insofar as it represents a particular example of repeatable patterns that have always occurred and will continue to do so forever. Because history is not linear, it has no "metanarrative," no comprehensive meaning that transcends all of history and brings together all the individual moments in time. A revolving wheel is often the image used to visually depict this philosophy of history.

Various versions of the cyclical view of history have frequently been popular in cultures that blur the lines between myths and real historical events. There are at least two related explanations for the origins of cyclical understandings of history. First, each cycle of history in some respects parallels the normal pattern of a human life. The individual experience was thus projected onto the historical process and incorporated into a never-ending cycle. The second explanation for this view is related to the agrarian milieu of many ancient civilizations. History was understood to be part of natural processes. In an agricultural context, people regularly observe the yearly cycle of seasons and how they affect sowing and reaping. In the cyclical view of history, the rhythm of nature was projected onto the larger historical process; the latter, in fact, was understood to be the source of the former. Cyclical history was the default interpretation of the past in the Greco-Roman world, the Middle East, the Far East, and India. A cyclical view of the past has often been coupled with a fatalistic understanding of the future.

---

[4] My discussion of the Eastern view is adapted from my essay "Eastern and New Age Views of History" in the *Christian Worldview Study Bible* (Nashville: B&H Reference, forthcoming). This material is used here with permission of the publisher.

Cyclical history is incompatible with the Christian worldview. The Bible argues that history is linear, moving from creation to consummation. Rather than being left to the purposeless powers of fate, history is in the hands of a purposeful God who providentially moves history forward to fulfill his sovereign purposes. In a cyclical view of history, the past—and present and future—have no real meaning. According to the Christian worldview, history is filled with meaning, even if we never fully grasp all the ways the Lord is working at any given moment. According to Bebbington, in Western culture, the Judeo-Christian understanding of history supplanted the cyclical view of history in the early Middle Ages, though the latter has been revived from time to time among individual historians such as Oswald Spengler (1880–1936) and Arnold Toynbee (1852–1883).[5] The cyclical view is also common in popular discussions of history, especially among those who interpret the past as a morality tale. As I mentioned briefly in the introduction, who has not heard that history repeats itself, in a bad way, when we do not learn the lessons the past teaches us? Nevertheless, modern professional historians almost uniformly embrace a linear understanding of history, even when they do not embrace a Christian worldview.

HISTORY AS PROGRESS

While Western culture is generally averse to cyclical fatalism, it has often taken a friendlier posture since the eighteenth century toward the concept of progress. Bebbington argues that "the idea of progress that emerged in the Enlightenment of the eighteenth century was a secularization of the Christian view of history."[6] The progress view maintains that the historical process is linear, but the theological rationale of the Judeo-Christian tradition is removed as humanity is increasingly considered the central player in a world that is

---

[5] David Bebbington, *Patterns in History: A Christian Perspective on Historical Thought* (Nottingham, UK: Inter-Varsity, 1979; repr., Vancouver, British Columbia: Regent College Publishing, 1990), 33–34, 37–39.

[6] Ibid., 68.

ever evolving from the primitive to the progressive. As the name suggests, this is an optimistic approach because its proponents affirmed things are always moving in the right direction, even if certain periods in the past represented temporary setbacks. Historians who emphasize progress tend to highlight what they consider to be the best ideas in the past, since it is these ideas they suggest that have contributed to their present context. History as progress reached its peak during the first quarter of the 20th century, when it was subsequently chastened by the atrocities of World War I.

The best-known interpretation of history that emphasizes progress is the so-called whig interpretation of history, a form of presentism that I referenced in the last chapter. By way of reminder, whig history, as critiqued by Herbert Butterfield, emphasized the inevitability of greater liberty, democracy, and enlightenment. Thomas Babington Macaulay's five-volume *History of England from the Accession of James the Second* (1848–1855) represents the most famous example of the whig interpretation of history. In America, an emphasis on progress came through the eighteenth-century English Enlightenment (especially the writings of John Locke) and influenced many of our nation's leading founders. In a real sense, a commitment to progress was woven into the very DNA of American culture. For this reason, American political and military history, particularly works written prior to the mid-twentieth century, assumed a progress interpretation of history that focused on American territorial expansion and the spread of republican ideas. Many popular historians and biographers, especially those who focus on the Revolutionary era and Early Republic of America such as David McCullough (b. 1933), Walter Isaacson (b. 1952), and Richard Brookhiser (b. 1955), emphasize the theme of progress in those Enlightenment values that they suggest were most dear to the Founding Fathers.[7]

---

[7] Michael Knox Beran suggests progress is making a comeback even among some contemporary academic historians. See Michael Knox Beran, "Whig History is Back," History News Network, accessed June 2, 2014, http://hnn.us/article/43723.

A progress view of history seems intuitive at some levels, but like all forms of presentism, it lacks sufficient nuance and fails to interpret the past on its own terms. It is also arrogant, even if implicitly, since the cherished values and assumptions of the present are assumed to be the best gauge of the past. Furthermore, for Christians in particular, the idea that history is progress becomes problematic when divorced from a Christian worldview. Who gets to decide what values and priorities represent true progress? Is this decision made by cultural elites, or the economically privileged, or the educated, or ethnic majorities? What of human sin? Have we progressed as far as we think if we can eradicate polio with vaccinations but pornography is more widely available through the Internet? To be sure, Christians believe in progress; God is sovereignly bringing about his good purposes from creation to consummation. But God's ways are not always our ways, and progress, even when discernible, must always be tempered with a robust understanding of human sinfulness. While perhaps preferable to a cyclical view of history, the progress view, at least in its most common forms, ultimately falls short of the mark for Christian historians.[8]

HISTORICISM

While progress has strongly influenced historical interpretation in Britain and North America, historicism has been more influential in continental Europe. Historicism is the belief that all cultures are determined by their history. Indeed, historical development is considered to be a fundamental aspect of human existence. Rather than focusing on the linear nature of history, historicism argues that the past should be interpreted differently in each culture because every culture is unique and thus developing in its own peculiar way. Historicism avoids any universal interpretations; all history is con-

---

[8] For a creative appropriation of the progress view from the perspective of the Christian worldview, see Wilfred M. McClay, "The Christian Historian and the Idea of Progress," in *Confessing History: Explorations in Christian Faith and the Historian's Vocation*, eds. John Fea, Jay Green, and Eric Miller (Notre Dame, IN: University of Notre Dame Press, 2010), 316–44.

textual. The great contribution of the German historicists to the wider discipline of history is the belief that history is a science and that certain methods should be developed to research, interpret, and assess the study of the past.

The most famous historian in the historicist school was Leopold von Ranke (1795–1886), whose 1824 book *History of the Latin and Teutonic Peoples from 1494 to 1514* is often marked as the beginning of the modern academic discipline of history. Ranke argued that primary sources should be determinative in historical interpretation and suggested that the purpose of historical research was not to mine the past for moral lessons but simply demonstrate what had happened. The study of the past is a virtue in and of itself. In the English-speaking world, R. G. Collingwood (1889–1943) argued for a form of historicism in his posthumously published *The Idea of History* (1946). Like Ranke, Collingwood suggested history is an end unto itself and should be divorced from contemporary moralizing: "It teaches us what man has done and thus what man is."[9]

Perhaps the most important historicist was the German philosopher Georg W. F. Hegel (1770–1831), who combined historicism with philosophical idealism in his dialectical approach to history.[10] Hegel's view often is summarized as the relationship between thesis, antithesis, and synthesis, though he did not use these terms himself. In Hegelian thought, you begin with a thesis, which he argued necessarily implies its opposite, or antithesis. The tension between the two is resolved by a synthesis, which in turn becomes a new thesis—a new starting place for inquiry. While this might sound complicated, when applied to history, Hegel simply argued that the historical process is comprised of successions of events that develop in conflict with one another. In his discussion

---

[9] Collingwood, *The Idea of History*, 10.
[10] For a helpful introduction to Hegel's thought, see Paul Redding, "Georg Wilhelm Friedrich Hegel," *Stanford Encyclopedia of Philosophy*, ed. Edward N. Zalta (2010), accessed June 2, 2014, http://plato.stanford.edu/entries/hegel/.

of Hegelian thought, John Warwick Montgomery gives the example of the French Revolution. The authoritarian monarchy of the ancien régime in France (thesis) gave rise to the anarchic, libertine French Revolution (antithesis), which ultimately resulted in the French Republic that combined elements of both the old monarchy and the revolutionary era (synthesis).[11]

Historicism has significantly influenced the discipline of history, often in positive ways. Historicism's emphasis on primary sources and historical contextualization are part and parcel of being a careful historian. However, elements of historicism are also incompatible with a Christian worldview. First of all, historicism tends to undermine the value of individuals in favor of the cultures of which those individuals are part. This undermines the biblical doctrine of the *imago dei*, the image of God, a belief that suggests the sanctity of each human person. Historicism also posits that beliefs are shaped by culture rather than vice versa. While all beliefs are culturally conditioned to varying degrees, beliefs also shape cultures. The Catholicism of medieval Christendom and the Nazi ideology of the Third Reich were each influenced by their cultural contexts, but they were also worldviews that influenced every aspect of their respective cultures. Finally, historicism so emphasizes cultural conditioning of beliefs and practices it provides no foundations from which to make moral judgments. This position is popular in our current postmodern milieu, which champions moral relativism, but the Bible teaches that God has an unchangeable moral law that is written on the human heart (Rom. 2:15) and clearly taught in the Scriptures (Ex. 20:1–21).

MARXIST HISTORY

Marxism, while normally identified with economics and politics, has also contributed an influential interpretation of history. Marx-

---

[11] John Warwick Montgomery, *The Shape of the Past: A Christian Response to Secular Philosophies of History*, 2nd ed. (Minneapolis: Bethany House, 1975), 71.

ism is, of course, identified with Karl Marx (1818–1883), the German philosopher whose *Communist Manifesto* (1848) and other writings so influenced world history for much of the past century and continues to influence certain cultures in the early years of the present century. Marx, who was influenced by Hegel, combined elements of progress and historicism and applied the insights to economics and politics. According to Bebbington, in Marx's view of the past, "the starting-point is that man is the maker of his own history."[12] In Marxism, human beings, and especially "the common man," create the historical process as they labor to satisfy their basic needs. "The essential form of human activity is therefore production."[13] History unfolds according to different epochs wherein human production is disrupted because of class tensions, resulting in cultural revolutions. Whereas Hegel had allowed a place for God (broadly conceived) to be behind the march of history, for Marx and other Marxists such as his colleague Friedrich Engels (1820–1895), historical interpretation is governed by a "dogmatic materialism" that leaves no place for the divine.[14]

Marxist historical interpretation became popular in the English-speaking world during the 1960s and 1970s. Many of these historians were originally devout Marxists and sometimes even members of the Communist Party. For example, Christopher Hill, one of the most prestigious historians of seventeenth-century British history, interpreted the English Civil War as a class struggle rather than a religio-political conflict in his influential book *The World Turned Upside Down: Radical Ideas During the English Revolution* (1972).[15] An erstwhile communist, Hill left the Communist Party of Great Britain after the Soviet Union crushed the

---

[12] Bebbington, *Patterns in History*, 121.

[13] Ibid., 122.

[14] Montgomery, *Shape of the Past*, 75. Hegel's understanding of God was not orthodox, though he considered himself to be a Christian. See Stanley J. Grenz and Roger E. Olson, *20th-Century Theology: God and the World in a Transitional Age* (Downers Grove, IL: IVP Academic, 1993), 31–39.

[15] Christopher Hill, *The World Turned Upside Down: Radical Ideas During the English Revolution*, rev. ed. (New York: Penguin, 1991).

Hungarian Revolution in 1956. In America, Eugene Genovese, an eminent historian of antebellum slavery, interpreted the relationship between slaves and their masters through a Marxist grid in his Bancroft Prize–winning book *Roll, Jordan, Roll: The World the Slaves Made* (1974).[16] Genovese later abandoned his Marxism, renounced atheism, and converted to Roman Catholicism in the mid-1990s.

While ideological Marxism has waned in the past generation, Marxist categories of interpretation continue to be popular among many social historians. In North America, social history arose in the context of 1960s campus radicalism. The so-called New Left influenced many historians to see themselves as social activists who used the past as a tool to bring about cultural change. For example, Howard Zinn's (1922–2010) best-selling book *A People's History of the United States* (1980), which focuses on women, minorities, and the marginalized, is strongly influenced by Marxist categories. Historians sympathetic to Marxism, as well as those who have embraced left-wing versions of progress, have also been key advocates of teaching social studies in public schools rather than traditional approaches to history.[17] Rather than focusing on major figures, themes, and events like most history classes, social studies entails "the integrated study of the social sciences and humanities to promote civic competence."[18] The discipline of social studies is dominated by a progressive and presentist agenda.

Marxist history is helpful to the degree that it reminds historians of the role that class conflict has often played in the past. Furthermore, especially in the twentieth century, many movements were self-consciously driven by class concerns, even when they were

---

[16] Eugene Genovese, *Roll, Jordan, Roll: The World the Slaves Made* (New York: Random House, 1974).

[17] John Fea, *Why Study History? Reflecting on the Importance of the Past* (Grand Rapids, MI: Baker Academic, 2013), 44–45.

[18] This is the definition advanced by the National Council of Social Studies, an organization dedicated to promoting the social studies in education. See "About National Council of Social Studies," National Council of Social Studies, accessed June 3, 2014, http://www.socialstudies.org/about.

not always uniformly communist; the modern labor movement comes to mind. That said, Marxist history, when embraced as an ideology, is ultimately incompatible with a Christian worldview because of the foundational role it assigns to class and economic production. Marxism has no explanatory power for concepts such as the true, the good, and the beautiful, because these ideas cannot be explained through a paradigm that believes concerns about production and the class conflict it generates lie at the heart of the human experience. Marxist history is only viable when atheism is assumed; Marx and Engel understood this in ways that some modern historians do not. Contra the atheistic determinism of Marxism, Christian historians believe that human agency and individual personalities and priorities are central to the unfolding of history. The Christian historian will learn from the Marxist view of history, but he or she cannot embrace it uncritically without abandoning the Christian worldview.

JUDEO-CHRISTIAN HISTORY

Historically, the Judeo-Christian approach to history reached its maturity around the same time the cyclical view was declining in the West. I have chosen to save it for last because it is so foundational to a book, such as this, that introduces students to the discipline of history from the perspective of a Christian worldview. According to Bebbington,

> Christians, then, have normally adhered to these three convictions about history: that God intervenes in it; that he guides it in a straight line; and that he will bring it to the conclusion that he has planned. The three beliefs together form the core of the Christian doctrine of providence.[19]

These convictions arise from the Bible, which depicts God as providentially reigning over all of creation, including the march of time.

---

[19] Bebbington, *Patterns in History*, 43.

Of course, God launches history in Genesis and brings it to a close in Revelation. But he also guides history in between. For example, in the Old Testament, Psalm 136 recounts the mighty acts of God from creation, to Israel's exodus from Egypt, to the rise and fall of kings, to his providential provision of food. The psalm begins and ends with a call to give thanks to the Lord, who is good, whose "steadfast love endures forever" (Ps. 136:1, 26). Israel's fortunes—and the fortunes of all the nations—were in the Lord's hands. In the New Testament, Galatians 4:4 claims that God "sent forth his Son" when "the fullness of time" had come. The incarnation took place at exactly the moment in history that God had providentially arranged.

The Bible presents history as both linear and teleological. History is linear because it moves sequentially from beginning to end. History is teleological in that the events are purposeful toward their ultimate end: the glory of God in the salvation of sinful humans and the redemption of the created order. Interestingly, the Old Testament sometimes presents history as cyclical. For example, the book of Judges is structured around cycles of decline, deliverance, prosperity, and decline. However, as John Warwick Montgomery points out, the biblical view of history, while cyclical at times, develops along a linear path from creation to consummation.[20] Even when cyclical, the sequential and purposeful biblical view of history stands in stark contrast to the fatalism of the Greco-Roman and Eastern views of history that were common during the periods that overlapped with the events recorded in the Scriptures.

Aside from the Bible, the earliest shapers of the Judeo-Christian view of history were Eusebius of Caesarea (ca. 260–340) and Augustine of Hippo (354–430). Eusebius contributed several important works that shaped the Christian intellectual tradition, though three particularly influenced the Judeo-Christian approach to

---

[20] Montgomery, *Shape of the Past*, 43–45.

history.[21] His *Ecclesiastical History* is the oldest-surviving comprehensive history of Christianity. Eusebius recounted church history from the time of Christ until around the year 325. He discussed the life of Christ, provided a succession of key bishops, countered heresies, and chronicled periods of persecution. For Eusebius, Christian history to that point had climaxed with the conversion of Constantine, an event discussed in great detail in Eusebius's *Life of Constantine*. Eusebius believed that God was in control of history and had orchestrated events in such a way to bring about the Christianization of the Roman Empire. Unlike many earlier theologians, but following the influential Origen of Alexandria (ca. 184–254), Eusebius rejected a literal future millennium and gradually downplayed the second coming in his writings. Instead, he optimistically advocated a spiritual understanding of the millennium that allowed him to closely identify the advance of God's kingdom with the increasingly Christianized Roman Empire. Eusebius's *Chronicle*, which followed the conventions of Roman historical writing, was a sweeping history of the world from Abraham to Constantine, though written from the perspective of Eusebius's Christian worldview.

Augustine's major contribution to the Christian view of history is found in his magnum opus, *The City of God*, which was written between 410 and 426.[22] When the Visigoths sacked Rome in 410, it crushed the optimism that had prevailed since the time of Eusebius. Some questioned whether Rome was being punished for abandoning its traditional religion in favor of Christianity. In *The City of God*, Augustine depicts human history as a conflict between the city of man and the city of God. Following the bibli-

---

[21] For more on Eusebius's view of history, see Timothy D. Barnes, *Constantine and Eusebius* (Cambridge, MA: Harvard University Press, 1981), 126–89, and Ernst Breisach, ed., *Historiography: Ancient, Medieval, and Modern*, 3rd ed. (Chicago: University of Chicago Press, 2007), 81–82.

[22] For an introduction to Augustine's philosophy of history and selections from *The City of God*, see Pardon E. Tillinghast, ed., *Approaches to History: Selections in the Philosophy of History from the Greeks to the Romans* (Englewood Cliffs, NJ: Prentice Hall, 1963), 57–83. See also Breisach, *Historiography*, 84–86.

cal storyline, Augustine believed the latter would ultimately prevail. According to this reckoning, the Roman Empire was not to be identified with God's kingdom; the empire was part of the city of man. The city of God was the elect of God, all the believers of all the ages, chosen by God for eternal life beyond this present earthly existence. This city of God included Roman believers—but only believers. Rome's fall, while tragic, does not mean the kingdom of God has been shaken. The city of God advances as human kingdoms rise and fall.

Augustine's view of history provided the basic mental scaffolding for the Judeo-Christian view of history in the West through the Enlightenment, though various thinkers tweaked it along the way. As a general rule, in the Middle Ages the city of God was identified with the Catholic Church while the city of man was identified with the secular realm and history; the former was considered far more important than the latter. Yet, some medieval thinkers made creative contributions to the Christian view of history. The Venerable Bede (673–735) offered a less Roman and more critical assessment of Christian history in his *Ecclesiastical History of the English People* (731). Joachim of Fiore (1135–1202) fused an apocalyptic view of the end times into his view of history and divided all of time into three ages: the age of the Father (pre-Christianity), the age of the Son (the Christian era), and the age of the Holy Spirit (the coming millennium). Renaissance historians emphasized the importance of critical study of primary sources, prefiguring the development of the modern discipline of history, while Reformation-era history tended to be polemical in nature, defending either Protestant movements or Catholicism as being the true representatives of the city of God. Throughout this period, history was closely identified with God's providence.[23]

In the post-Reformation period, as the Enlightenment chal-

---

[23] Bebbington, *Patterns in History*, 56–64; Breisach, *Historiography*, 121–37, 153–70; Montgomery, *Shape of the Past*, 45–52.

lenged the Christian worldview, the progress view and historicism supplanted the Judeo-Christian view of history. For the emerging class of professional historians, history was no longer a theological and ethical discipline, but rather was considered a science. Many Protestant and Catholic historians who felt strongly about the doctrine of providence focused their attention on church history, which also became a formal discipline in the nineteenth century, but which tended to be written for believers rather than the academic community until well into the twentieth century. From time to time, academic historians attempted to integrate their Christian faith into their understanding of history. Notable examples include the British Methodist Herbert Butterfield (1900–1979), the American Baptist Kenneth Scott Latourette (1884–1968), and the British Catholic Christopher Dawson (1888–1970).[24] It was not until the 1960s that Christian historians began to reflect in increasingly serious ways about the relationship between faith and history. This will be the subject of chapter 3. However, first we need to discuss the topic of historiography.

HISTORIOGRAPHY

Every historian has a particular view of history, whether he or she knows it or not. Even so, one's approach to history comprises only one aspect of historical interpretation. In the introduction, we discussed how historians work with both primary and secondary sources. While the former should be the basis of our understanding of the past, this is aided by our familiarity with the latter. Good historians study, interact with, and build upon the interpretations of earliest historians who have studied the same subjects and related topics. According to Jules Benjamin, "historiography . . . examines changes in the methods, interpretations, and conclusions

---

[24] See Herbert Butterfield, *Christianity and History* (London: Bell and Sons, 1949); Kenneth Scott Latourette, "The Christian Understanding of History," *American Historical Review* 54, no. 2 (January 1949): 259–67; Christopher Dawson, *Religion and the Rise of Western Culture* (London: Sheed & Ward, 1950).

of earlier generations of historians."[25] Over time, reigning interpretations are nuanced and sometimes even rejected outright as
historians build upon the work of their predecessors. As we learned
in the last chapter, all historians are revisionists; this is because the
historiography of any given topic is always being advanced as new
historians tackle the past.

It is impossible to interpret history without a grasp of historiography. As one introduction to history argues,

> Historians read secondary sources to develop a sense of back-
> ground, historical context, historiographical context, and to un-
> derstand the author's central argument and use of sources. . . .
> Having a sense of historiography can help the reader understand
> why interpretations, methodology, and scholarly approaches
> have evolved.[26]

Understanding the "history of the history" of your subject provides important nuance needed to properly interpret a subject. Our
understanding of nearly every topic from the past has evolved over
time as new scholars contribute to the historiography of a particular field. This is especially the case when different approaches to
history complement one another. Often, social historians, intellectual historians, and cultural historians offer competing interpretations of the past. Careful historians will build upon the insights of
each of these subdisciplines (and others) to arrive at as comprehensive an interpretation of the past as possible. Even then, historians
should be humble enough to admit they have almost certainly not
written the last word on their subject.

I first learned the importance of historiography in a college
class on the Old South, taught by a young historian fresh out of his
doctoral studies at the University of Southern Mississippi. When
we discussed slavery, Dr. Robins talked about how historical in-

---

[25] Benjamin, *Student's Guide to History*, 7.
[26] Michael J. Galgano, J. Chris Arndt, and Raymond M. Hyser, *Doing History: Research and Writing
in the Digital Age* (Belmont, CA: Wadsworth Cengage, 2008), 42.

terpretations had changed over time. In 1929, U. B. Phillips had argued that slavery was unprofitable but had been maintained as an institution because it civilized African Americans.[27] Phillips, writing as a white southerner in the middle of the Jim Crow era, advanced a paternalistic interpretation of slavery. In 1956, Kenneth Stampp challenged Phillips's interpretation.[28] Stampp, writing on the heels of the *Brown v. Board of Education* Supreme Court decision, argued that slavery was not paternalistic and unprofitable, but rather was exploitative, harsh, and profitable. Three years later, Stanley Elkins focused on the psychological impact of slavery, comparing the brutal treatment of slaves to the Nazi abuse of Jews in concentration camps.[29] Eugene Genovese, in his aforementioned *Roll, Jordan, Roll* (1974), argued that slavery was a way of life for most southerners, that slaves had their own culture that existed alongside white culture, and suggested that slaves exercised passive resistance against their masters. Historians who study slavery must build upon the insights of these classics and hundreds of other books, articles, and dissertations, if they are to understand slavery in antebellum America.

When a Christian historian interacts with the historiographical literature on a particular topic, it must be out of the same spirit of neighbor-love that should guide our engagement with primary sources. We should give our fellow historians the benefit of the doubt and engage their arguments as charitably as possible, even when we might strongly disagree with their interpretations. Furthermore, the biblical admonition to be truth tellers as well as the scholarly conventions of professional history should motivate us to give other historians credit for their interpretations. Plagiarism remains a constant temptation; sometimes, even honest historians

---

[27] Ulrich Bonnell Phillips, *Life and Labor in the Old South* (Boston: Little, Brown and Company, 1929).

[28] Kenneth Stampp, *The Peculiar Institution: Slavery in the Ante-Bellum South* (New York: Vintage, 1956).

[29] Stanley M. Elkins, *Slavery: A Problem in American Institutional and Intellectual Life* (Chicago: University of Chicago Press, 1959).

inadvertently parrot the interpretations of others because they have not done due diligence in familiarizing themselves with the relevant secondary sources. Careful Christian historians should interact with other historians in a comprehensive and winsome manner out of a desire to honor the work of others, contribute to our knowledge of the past, and ultimately to honor God with the excellence of our labors. For the Christian historian in particular, contributing to the historiography of a subject in the right way and for the right reasons should be more important than simply making a contribution.

✚ 3

FAITH AND THE HISTORIAN

Within the scholarly realm that is here in question [the historian] is not allowed to bring God into the argument, or to pretend to use him as a witness, any more than a scientist, explaining a blade of grass under a microscope, is allowed to bring God into his explanations of the growth or decay of plants. . . . And the historian seeks the historical explanation of what happened, just as the physicist will give a scientific explanation of what has happened in his laboratory. Both historian and scientist offer a partial explanation—each in his own terms—but not by any means a total explanation of anything.[1]

Herbert Butterfield

One of the thorniest questions facing Christian historians is the relationship between their faith and their scholarship. A few months before I began writing this chapter, I was invited to participate in a discussion on this topic with colleagues at a different institution from the one where I teach. The participants included professional historians teaching in academic institutions, local church ministers who had pursued graduate studies in history, and doctoral students training for one or the other (or both) of these occupations. It did not take long to discern that our little group enjoyed no consensus on the question of how faith relates to the discipline of history. Some participants argued that, for the believer, academic history

---

[1] Herbert Butterfield, "Does Belief in Christianity Validly Affect the Modern Historian?" in *Herbert Butterfield: Writings on Christianity and History*, ed. C. T. McIntire (New York: Oxford University Press, 1979), 134.

should be a subdiscipline of theology because God providentially controls all things. Others argued that history is a discipline unto itself with certain rules and expectations by which all historians, including Christians, should abide. Still others argued that context, such as audience or intended readership, affects how the Christian historian interprets his or her subject. Our conversation was a microcosm of a larger discussion that has been taking place among Christian historians since at least the 1960s.

PROVIDENCE AND HISTORY

Until the late 1800s, it was common for Christian historians to adopt what is sometimes called a "providentialist" interpretation of history. According to the providentialist approach, the task of the historian is to discern God's guiding hand in the events of history. Not surprisingly, religious history was often interpreted along these lines. For example, Philip Schaff, the influential nineteenth-century church historian, argued, "A view of history which overlooks or undervalues the divine factor starts from deism and consistently runs into atheism."[2] He further suggested that, "The history of the church is the rise and progress of the kingdom of heaven upon earth, for the glory of God and the salvation of the world."[3] Interestingly, historians who wrote on nonreligious topics also often adopted the providentialist view. John Fea argues that many of the leading nineteenth-century historicists such as Leopold von Ranke in Germany and George Bancroft in the United States wrote with an eye to the forward march of divine providence. For many of the providence-minded historicists, "[God's] divine mission proved to be a significant motivating factor, even an inspiration, for doing historical work."[4]

---

[2] Philip Schaff, *History of the Christian Church, vol. 1: Apostolic Christianity: From the Birth of Christ to the Death of St. John, A.D. 1–100* (New York: Charles Scribner's Sons, 1858; repr., Peabody, MA: Hendrickson, 2002), 2.
[3] Ibid., 3.
[4] John Fea, *Why Study History? Reflecting on the Importance of the Past* (Grand Rapids, MI: Baker Academic, 2013), 70.

Providentialist history became increasingly passé with the rise of the modern historical profession during the latter decades of the nineteenth century. Rather than operating from explicitly Christian assumptions, professional historians increasingly operated from more naturalistic presuppositions. Gradually, most historians not only downplayed or rejected Christian presuppositions in their own work, but they also largely ignored the role of Christian faith—or any other religious commitments—in human actions. Timothy Larsen suggests two reasons for the marginalization of Christianity from historical interpretation. First, the secularization thesis, which was popular among historians and social scientists during the latter half of the twentieth century, argued that religion decreased in proportion to the modernization of a society. Second, Marxism, with its atheistic assumptions, emerged as a major influencer among professional historians.[5] For the most part, professional historians ignored providence, though as mentioned in the previous chapter, there were occasional exceptions to this general trend.

Throughout the twentieth century, some Christian historians, especially church historians who studied their own denominational traditions, continued to embrace the providentialist paradigm, though research standards were often greatly improved from the work of previous centuries as denominational historians increasingly embraced the standards of the broader academy.[6] And, of course, providentialism remained dominant at the popular level where history was often understood to be explicitly for the purpose of moral and spiritual formation. But by the late 1960s, a growing number of Christian historians began attempting to chart a course between the secularist assumptions of the academy and the providentialist

---

[5] Timothy Larsen, "Evangelicals, the Academy, and the Discipline of History," in *Beyond Integration? Inter/Disciplinary Possibilities for the Future of Christian Higher Education*, eds. Todd C. Ream, Jerry Pattengale, and David L. Riggs (Abilene, TX: Abilene Christian University Press, 2012), 105–6.
[6] See Keith Harper, ed., *American Denominational History: Perspectives on the Past, Prospects for the Future*, Religion & American Culture (Tuscaloosa, AL: University of Alabama Press, 2008).

convictions of popular Christian historians. In 1967, a group of evangelical historians established the Conference on Faith and History (CFH) as an auxiliary to the mainstream American Historical Association. Since that time, the CFH, which has broadened over the years to include many Roman Catholics, has emerged as the premier venue through which believing historians discuss the very matters under consideration in this chapter. The organization's journal, *Fides et Historia*, regularly addresses the relationship between faith, historical interpretation, the academy, and the church. In addition to the journal, two anthologies have been published that reprint key essays from *Fides et Historia*.[7] The CFH also proved influential in the development of the so-called new evangelical historiography.

In the 1980s and 1990s, several evangelical historians began to gain greater prominence within the historical profession. George Marsden, Mark Noll, Nathan Hatch, Harry Stout, Edith Blumhofer, Joel Carpenter, and Grant Wacker, in America, along with George Rawlyk in Canada and David Bebbington in Great Britain, published dozens of major monographs and hundreds of articles with some of the most prestigious publishers and journals in the profession. These scholars, along with the graduate students they trained, managed to combine a strong personal faith with the highest standards of historical scholarship.[8] Noll and Marsden also wrote on the nature of Christian scholarship itself. In *The Scandal of the Evangelical Mind* (1995), Noll laments that evangelicals in particular have not historically championed serious scholarship

---

[7] See George Marsden and Frank Roberts, eds., *A Christian View of History?* (Grand Rapids, MI: Eerdmans, 1975); and C. T. McIntire and Ronald A. Wells, eds., *History and Historical Understanding* (Grand Rapids, MI: Eerdmans, 1984).

[8] For a journalistic account of this trend, see Tim Stafford, "Whatever Happened to Christian History?" *Christianity Today*, April 2, 2001, accessed July 23, 2014, http://www.christianitytoday.com/ct/2001/april2/whatever-happened-to-christian-history.html?paging=off. For a historical assessment of the new evangelical historiography written by a movement insider, see David W. Bebbington, "The Evangelical Discovery of History," in *The Church on its Past: Papers Read at the 2011 Summer Meeting and 2012 Winter Meeting of the Ecclesiastical History Society*, eds. Peter D. Clarke and Charlotte Methuen (Martlesham, Suffolk, UK: Boydell, 2013), 330–64. See also Maxie B. Burch, *The Evangelical Historians: The Historiography of George Marsden, Nathan Hatch, and Mark Noll* (Lanham, MD: University Press of America, 1996).

and called for a renewed commitment to serious engagement with the academic disciplines. In *The Outrageous Idea of Christian Scholarship* (1998), Marsden argues that a truly pluralistic academy, which would be open to any viewpoint rigorously and credibly argued, should allow explicitly Christian voices to have a seat at the table.

These evangelical historians were not old-fashioned providentialists, though sometimes secularist colleagues accused them of such.[9] Though they certainly believed in God's providence, they worked within the naturalistic parameters of the historical discipline and were hesitant to assign divine causation to historical events. Their Christian faith was evident, not in any attempt to fashion history into a sermon, but rather in how they approached their discipline. For example, Marsden argues his faith affects the topics he chooses to study (he is a historian of American Christianity), the questions he asks (he assumes religion really mattered to the subjects he studies), and which theories he accepts (as a Christian, he rejects radical postmodernism).[10] Timothy Larsen, a protégé of Noll and Bebbington, adds that his own Christian faith causes him to sympathize with his subjects (he understands their religious presuppositions) and avoid sweeping reductionist explanations that dismiss the supernatural and unseen (more goes on than what the historian can assess based on the available evidence).[11]

This willingness to embrace what Larsen calls "methodological naturalism" has at times elicited strong criticism from Christians committed to a providentialist approach to history.[12] According to providentialists, for a Christian to hesitate to interpret God's workings in history is to embrace a professional atheism and to "sell out" to the unbelieving world. In the same way that the Bible

[9] Bruce Kuklick, "On Critical History," in *Religious Advocacy and American History*, eds. Bruce Kuklick and D. G. Hart (Grand Rapids, MI: Eerdmans, 1997), 54–64.
[10] George M. Marsden, "What Differences Might Christian Perspectives Make?" in *History and the Christian Historian*, ed. Ronald A. Wells (Grand Rapids, MI: Eerdmans, 1998), 15–16.
[11] Larsen, "Evangelicals," 114–15.
[12] Ibid., 110.

provides a theological account for the history it covers, Christian historians are to provide a theological account for the history they study. The most famous debate about the relationship between providence and history occurred in the early 1990s. The occasion for the debate was a study related to a particularly difficult phenomenon for nonprovidentialist historians to interpret: religious revival and spiritual awakening.

In 1991, Harry Stout, an evangelical historian who teaches at Yale University, published a biography of the famous evangelist George Whitefield titled *The Divine Dramatist: George Whitefield and the Rise of Modern Evangelicalism*.[13] Stout attributed much of Whitefield's success to his preconversion preparation to be an actor and his skills in marketing and promotion. Since Stout did not have access to God's personal thoughts about Whitefield, this is what he believed could be discerned about the revivalist based upon the evidence that was available. Some observers believed Stout took on a far too skeptical tone in his biography. In response to *The Divine Dramatist*, Iain Murray, a minister and popular historian and biographer with a keen interest in revival, charged Stout with adopting anti-Christian presuppositions and painting a grossly inaccurate portrait of Whitefield.[14] Almost twenty years after Stout's biography appeared, pastor and popular biographer John Piper raised the issue once more. Piper claimed Stout's biography "is the most sustained piece of historical cynicism I have ever read. In the first one hundred pages of this book, I wrote the word cynical in the margin seventy times."[15]

In my own experience, many Christian students who read

---

[13] Harry S. Stout, *The Divine Dramatist: George Whitefield and the Rise of Modern Evangelicalism*, Library of Religious Biography (Grand Rapids, MI: Eerdmans, 1991).

[14] For more on this debate and its effects, see D. G. Hart, "History in Search of Meaning: The Conference on Faith and History," in *History and the Christian Historian*, ed. Wells, 68–71, 85–87; and Andrew Atherstone, "Hagiography and History," in *Truth at Any Cost: Papers Read at the 2012 Westminster Conference* (Stoke-on-Trent, Staffordshire, UK: Tentmaker, 2012), 43–51.

[15] John Piper, "'I Will Not Be a Velvet-Mouthed Preacher!' The Life and Ministry of George Whitefield: Living and Preaching as Though God Were Real (Because He Is)," (biographical address, Desiring God National Pastor's Conference, 2009), accessed October 3, 2014, http://www.desiring god.org/messages/i-will-not-be-a-velvet-mouthed-preacher.

Stout's biography have a similar reaction to Murray and Piper because Stout does not argue that the Holy Spirit used Whitefield as a catalyst in the First Great Awakening. My students do not like that Stout is not writing about a major Christian figure for the specific purpose of moral and spiritual formation. My own views are mixed. While I appreciate that Stout did not write a "hagiography"—a pious biography intended to bless readers spiritually—I am concerned he went too far in his naturalistic tone. It is one thing to not attribute all of Whitefield's ministry success to the power of the Holy Spirit; it is another thing entirely to attribute so much of Whitefield's success to natural factors that you functionally preclude that the Holy Spirit was at work in his ministry. Arguably, Stout does the latter, though because he is a Christian, I assume Stout personally believes the Spirit to have been at work in Whitefield's ministry.[16]

More recently, in the wake of the 9/11 terrorist attacks in America, Steven Keillor has argued that Christian historians should not be so hesitant to discern God's judgment in certain historical circumstances.[17] Unlike Murray, Keillor is a trained historian who has published scholarly monographs and taught at academic institutions. Some historians, both Protestant and Catholic, have expressed appreciation for Keillor's provocative thesis, though without actually embracing Keillor's views.[18] I believe Keillor raises good questions that are worth reflecting upon; serious Christians believe that God's judgment for sins, both personal and corporate, is an awful reality. That said, I am hesitant as a historian to make

---

[16] In his recent scholarly biography of Whitefield, Baylor University historian Thomas Kidd offers a critical assessment of Whitefield's life and ministry and refuses to whitewash Whitefield's shortcomings. Nevertheless, he assumes Whitefield was sincere in his religious beliefs and does not write in such a way that he precludes, even implicitly, that the Lord used Whitefield to help bring religious revival to the American colonies. See Thomas S. Kidd, *George Whitefield: America's Spiritual Founding Father* (New Haven, CT: Yale University Press, 2014).

[17] Steven J. Keillor, *God's Judgments: Interpreting History and the Christian Faith* (Downers Grove, IL: IVP Academic, 2007).

[18] See Fea, *Why Study History?*, 71–72; and Brad S. Gregory, "The Lord Shall Judge," *Books & Culture: A Christian Review*, July/August 2007, accessed July 23, 2014, http://www.booksandculture.com/articles/2007/julaug/5.18.html?paging=off.

"prophetic" pronouncements about how God might be judging specific people or nations through particular events.

Historians have been less appreciative of the providentialist interpretations of David Barton, a minister and political activist who argues that America was founded as a Christian nation and that most of the Founding Fathers themselves were orthodox evangelicals. Barton, who is not a trained historian, claims that "revisionist" scholars have distorted the past by secularizing the Founding Fathers. While Barton's writings are very popular with some on the right wing of the political spectrum, historians have pointed out that Barton uses flawed research methods to bolster his providentialist argument.[19] In 2013, a group of thirty-three Christian historians wrote a letter to the Family Research Council asking them to remove a video of Barton giving a tour of the US Capitol from their YouTube channel because of its historical inaccuracies; the organization initially agreed to do so, though in spring 2014 Barton again led a tour of the Capitol for a Family Research Council event.[20]

In a very real sense, this is a discussion about how Christian historians should interpret religious history—especially (though not exclusively) religion in the United States.[21] At the moment, historians are not debating a Christian historical interpretation of nineteenth-century immigration in France or twentieth-century Japanese political history. For that matter, historians are not even debating a Christian interpretation of some topics overtly influenced by religion such as the abolition of slavery in the British Empire or South African apartheid. Because many historians choose

---

[19] See John Fea, *Was America Founded as a Christian Nation?* (Louisville, KY: Westminster-John Knox, 2011), 57–75. This chapter also discusses other providentialist popular historians of America's founding.

[20] Warren Throckmorton, who took the lead in challenging Barton's video, reported on these incidents on his personal blog. See http://www.patheos.com/blogs/warrenthrockmorton/2013/05/07/citing-historical-errors-frc-removes-david-bartons-capitol-tour-video/ (accessed October 3, 2014), and http://www.patheos.com/blogs/warrenthrockmorton/2014/05/30/david-barton-back-in-good-graces-of-family-research-council/ (accessed October 3, 2014). In the interest of full disclosure, I was one of the thirty-three historians who signed the 2013 letter to the Family Research Council.

[21] I am grateful to John Wilsey for pointing out how often the providentialism debate is closely tied to the wider discussion of the history of Christianity in America.

to study topics that interest them on a personal level, it is not surprising that many Christian historians would choose to write about topics in religious history. Many nonreligious historians also focus on this topic. According to the American Historical Association, religious history has become the most popular field of expertise among its members.[22] For the foreseeable future, it is important for every Christian historian to be familiar with this discussion, even if it seems less directly relevant to his or her particular research interests.

THE CHRISTIAN WORLDVIEW AND HISTORICAL INTERPRETATION

As a Christian, I find a providentialist approach to history appealing in some respects. God is in control, and I want everyone to know it! Nevertheless, I do not believe that professional historians who are believers should adopt a providentialist approach to history. I take this position for two major reasons. First, though I am a strong believer in the doctrine of God's providence, I am also a strong believer in the doctrine of human finiteness. While God is working in all things to accomplish his perfect will according to his sovereign design for the sake of his own glory (Ps. 33:11; Rev. 4:11), we do not see into God's mind and discern his ways unless he reveals them to us (Deut. 29:29; Rom. 11:33–36). God has certainly provided us with the "big picture" of history in the Scriptures. Yet, in the case of nonbiblical history, God has not told us how to interpret individual events that occur. To act as though he has given us this gift is to confuse the vocations of theologian (or prophet!) and historian.

Second, how a given providentialist interprets history is necessarily colored by his or her particular presuppositions—both

---

[22] Robert B. Townsend, "A New Found Religion? The Field Surges among AHA Members," *Perspectives on History*, December 2009, accessed July 23, 2014, http://www.historians.org/publications-and-directories/perspectives-on-history/december–2009/a-new-found-religion-the-field-surges-among-aha-members.

theological and cultural. For example, activists such as David Barton and other providentialists (most of whom are ministers rather than trained historians) believe that America was founded as a Christian nation with a holy purpose because some of our earliest settlers were devout Protestants who believed, "Blessed is the nation whose God is the LORD, the people whom he has chosen as his heritage" (Ps. 33:12).[23] I understand why this argument resonates with many American believers. But what about the British Christian providentialist historian who counters, "Let every person be subject to the governing authorities. For there is no authority except from God, and those that exist have been instituted by God" (Rom. 13:1)? Would our British friend agree that God led the Founding Fathers to break away from England—a Christian nation!—and found the United States? I doubt it. (John Wesley sure did not take this view in the 1770s and 1780s!)

This same principle about presuppositions applies to religious history. Timothy Larsen points out that many of the same critics who grumble about nonprovidentialist interpretations of the First Great Awakening tend to dismiss providentialist accounts of the Azusa Street Revival of 1906. The latter birthed the Pentecostal movement in America. Because many of the providentialists who resonate with the First Great Awakening do not agree with Pentecostal beliefs, they do not apply their providentialist paradigm to the Azusa Street Revival. When considering this phenomenon, Larsen perceptively suggests that providentialist history "is a form of discourse that is limited to making applications for people who already think exactly like the author."[24]

Rather than adopting a providentialist approach to history,

---

[23] For examples of providentialist accounts of American history, see Peter Marshall and David Manuel, *The Light and the Glory: Did God Have a Plan for America?* (Grand Rapids, MI: Revell, 1977); Gary DeMar, *America's Christian Heritage* (Nashville: B&H, 2003); D. James Kennedy and Jerry Newcombe, *What if America Were a Christian Nation Again?* (Nashville: Thomas Nelson, 2003). For a similar account that is less overtly evangelical, see Larry Schweikart and Michael Allen, *A Patriot's History of the United States: From Columbus's Great Discovery to the War on Terror* (New York: Sentinel, 2004).

[24] Larsen, "Evangelicals," 111–12. The quote is found on page 111.

Christian historians would do better to look for ways that the Christian faith can be brought to bear on the historian's craft without taking on the mantle of the theologian or prophet. Marsden and Larsen make some helpful suggestions along these lines, which I referenced in the previous section. I would add that the Christian faith should help historians to exercise interpretive restraint. This posture can be somewhat countercultural; many historians at least give the impression that they believe they have the past all figured out. Christian humility ought to shatter this illusion. Providentialists, whether intentionally or not, at the very least imply that they understand the mind of God on historical matters. They tend to provide neat and tidy interpretations wherein almost everything that happens in history—which they approve of, at least—is the direct work of the Holy Spirit. Their claims, while pious, do not line up with reality. Of course, many secularist historians make this same mistake from a different direction by ignoring how religion (Christian or otherwise) often motivates adherents as much as, if not more than, other factors.

As we discussed in chapter 1, good historians understand that all historical interpretations are both provisional and incomplete. Unlike the providentialist or secularist, Christian historians in particular ought to own this truth and abandon the futile quest for permanent, complete, unassailable interpretations. Historians never glimpse the complete picture. Intuitively, I think we know this to be true. For example, in our own personal experiences, we understand there is much information we are not privy to, whether the innermost thoughts of other people, events happening in other places, or the invisible, spiritual realm around us. This is even more so the case when we study the past. Remember what we learned in the first chapter? The past is a foreign country.

Christian thinkers have historically distinguished between God's special revelation and his general revelation. Special revelation includes the various ways that God discloses knowledge of himself through supernatural means, including miracles, prophesies, and the inspired Scriptures (2 Tim. 3:16; Heb. 1:1–2). When theologians go about their task, they work primarily with information available through special revelation—especially the Bible. General revelation includes the various ways that God discloses knowledge of himself through natural means, including nature and conscience (Ps. 19:1–2; Rom. 1:19–20). Historians work within the realm of general revelation, assessing and interpreting evidence that is available to anyone, regardless of his or her religious beliefs. For a Christian historian to focus exclusively on evidence available through general revelation does not mean he or she need reject a firm belief in the supernatural, including special revelation. Far from it! However, recognizing that historians work with evidence available in general revelation rather than special revelation does mean we must always remember that it is not the historian's task to search for a "thus saith the Lord" in the realm of history. This is the critical mistake providentialists make, regardless of the quality of their personal faith.

In the introduction, I briefly introduced the concept of the Christian worldview and made some preliminary suggestions about ways it impacts the work of the historian. The time has come now to explain the Christian worldview in more explicit detail and apply it more concretely to the historian's work. First, I will discuss the only authoritative source for understanding the Christian worldview. Then, I will draw on two Christian traditions that are particularly helpful in fleshing out the relationship between the Christian worldview and the practice of history. The Reformed tradition, especially in its Dutch variation, provides us with a helpful summary of the Christian worldview that can be applied to the historian's task, whereas the Lutheran tradition offers us a helpful concept for envisioning the vocation of the historian.

All Christians believe that the Christian worldview should arise from the Bible. As Albert Wolters argues, "our worldview must be shaped and tested by Scripture. It can legitimately guide our lives only if it is scriptural."[25] The Dutch Reformed tradition helps us to understand that our worldview is best shaped by the storyline of Scripture. This approach has become so common that many American evangelicals who are not adherents of Dutch "neo-Calvinism" have adopted this way of discussing the Christian worldview. The grand biblical narrative, which develops from Genesis to Revelation, is unified and coherent. It recounts for us the story of the gospel and presents us with the lens through which we should view all of life. The biblical storyline can be divided into four key "movements": creation, fall, redemption, and restoration. Each of these movements centers upon historical events that carry theological and ethical ramifications. Each also has some bearing upon a Christian view of history.

The Biblical storyline begins with creation: "In the beginning, God created the heavens and the earth" (Gen. 1:1). In terms of the Christian worldview, creation points to at least two important realities. First, as Creator, God is the sovereign Lord who rules over everything he has created. According to Psalm 103:19, "The LORD has established his throne in the heavens, and his kingdom rules over all." He cares about the minutest details of this world: "Are not two sparrows sold for a penny? And not one of them will fall to the ground apart from your Father" (Matt. 10:29). Far from downplaying the doctrine of providence, the Christian historian is invigorated by a strong commitment to God's reign: everything matters to God because he is the Lord of all creation who rules according to his will. This includes the past, present, and future. As historians, we interpret the past through evidence available in general revelation to see many of the ways that God is at work around us in the ordinary details of this life.

Second, creation teaches us that human beings in particular are

---

[25] Albert M. Wolters, *Creation Regained: Biblical Basics for a Reformational Worldview*, 2nd ed. (Grand Rapids, MI: Eerdmans, 2005), 7.

created in God's image (Gen. 1:27). We reflect God's nature and purposes in a way that is not true of other creatures. Furthermore, God shows common grace to all those who are created in his image, whether Christian or not. In Matthew 5:45b, Jesus says, "For [God] makes his sun rise on the evil and on the good, and sends rain on the just and on the unjust." The doctrines of the *imago dei* ("image of God") and common grace mean that every individual and every human deed is inherently valuable in God's eyes. For the historian, every topic related to human beings and their various exploits—good, bad, and ugly—is inherently worthy of historical inquiry.

Speaking of the bad and ugly, the second moment in the grand biblical narrative is the fall. Genesis 3 teaches us that God's good creation has gone awry because of human sin. All people begin their lives in a state of rebellion against their rightful Lord. The apostle Paul reminds us, "all have sinned and fall short of the glory of God" (Rom. 3:23). The entire created order has been corrupted by human sin and stands in need of redemption and renewal (Rom. 8:19–22). Of course, each of us keenly understands this aspect of the Christian worldview because we know our own sinful tendencies and we see evidence of the sins of others all around us. The fall is relevant to historians, for as Marsden points out, "Of all traditional Christian teachings the doctrine of original sin or of pervasive human depravity has the most empirical verification."[26] It does not take long for a historian to be confronted with the reality of sin. It typically just takes a single trip to the archives.

Christian historians will understand that our subjects' actions, attitudes, and even motivations (which we are never fully privy to, if at all) will always be messy and therefore often belie simplistic interpretations because sin has bent every aspect of human existence. Furthermore, the reality that we live in a sinful world and are ourselves tainted by sin should remind us that there are limitations

---

[26] George M. Marsden, "Human Depravity: A Neglected Explanatory Category," in *Figures in the Carpet: Finding the Human Person in the American Past*, ed. Wilfed M. McClay (Grand Rapids, MI: Eerdmans, 2007), 16.

to what we can understand about the past. As Mark Noll argues, "The doctrine of the Fall and the resultant depravity of human nature suggests that the human moral condition obscures vision, presumably for historical as well as moral reasoning."[27] This provides yet another reason for historians to remain humble in our interpretations of the past. Not only do we not know everything, but what we do understand is filtered through the effects of the fall. Everything matters to God, but only God knows everything.

The third moment in the Bible's storyline is redemption, which points to how God has acted decisively through the person and work of Christ to fix everything that has been broken by human sin. Redemption is personal for those who believe in Jesus Christ (John 3:16; Titus 2:11–14) and cosmic as Christ's saving work extends to the natural order (Rom. 8:18–25). The movement in Scripture is from ruin to redemption. Christians consider this to be good news—*gospel*. As Christian historians, redemption reminds us that people, institutions, and even nations really can change. If the fall helps to keep us realistic in our interpretations, redemption (and, for that matter, common grace) helps prevent us from being overly cynical in how we interpret history. Unlike naturalistic determinists who assume all of life is fixed by natural causes and ultimately unchangeable, we believe that God is fixing what is broken. The doctrines of both sin and redemption help prevent us from putting the subjects of our study into predetermined "boxes" and empowers us to do our very best to empathize with the past in all of its manifold complications, and mutations, and plot twists.

The final moment in the grand biblical narrative is restoration, which is what will happen when redemption "goes viral." Revelation 21 and 22 show us that one day the work of redemption will be completed and God will reign once again over a fully

---

[27] Mark Noll, "Traditional Christianity and the Possibility of Historical Knowledge," in *Religious Advocacy and American History*, eds. Bruce Kuklick and D. G. Hart (Grand Rapids, MI: Eerdmans, 1997), 45–46.

redeemed cosmos populated by fully redeemed people. God's end game for his creation is everlasting flourishing under his perfect reign. Believing historians should be humbled by the reality of redemption and the promise of the world to come. Even what we believe to be the best of history pales in comparison to what the future holds. The reality of restoration should help Christian historians to avoid the temptation to see any moment in the past as a golden age. While secularist professional historians rarely gravitate toward overly sunny views of the past (their worldviews take them in different directions), many popular and/or providentialist historians commit this error. Restoration reminds us that the only golden age we should look to is the world to come. This frees us to treat the past on its own terms, whatever those might be for any given subject.

Whereas the Dutch Reformed tradition provides us with a helpful paradigm for understanding how the Christian worldview relates to the historian's craft, the Lutheran tradition can help us to apply that worldview to the historian's vocation. By using the word "vocation," I am not narrowly referring to the historian's occupation. Rather, I am speaking to the specific calling to be a historian, which may or may not be one's actual job (in terms of paying the bills). I would suggest that Christian historians should understand their training, ability, interests, and opportunities to exercise these things as one of their callings from the Lord. When the historian understands his work as part of his calling, he recognizes that work possesses an inherent worth that allows him to avoid the temptation to "redeem" history by attempting to make it theological, prophetic, or activist. History is a worthwhile pursuit in and of itself, especially by the Christian who does so unto God's glory.

To some readers, this might seem like a strange way to speak of calling. For many Christians, God's calling is only ever applied to vocational ministries such as pastoral work, foreign missions, or campus ministry. This has been a frequent mistake in Christian history. During the medieval era, it was common for the Catholic Church to use the language of calling only when referring to the two occupations of priest and monk. This painted a picture wherein most Christians are spiritually ordinary, but a few are spiritual "all-stars" because they have a special calling from God. During the Reformation, Martin Luther challenged this idea with his doctrine of *vocatio*, from which we get our English word "vocation." Luther argued that God was active in every occupation, every station in life, every responsibility, and when these different vocations or callings are undertaken out of love for God and neighbor, we are doing the Lord's work in our unique contexts. Luther believed that God calls some individuals like him to become full-time paid ministers, but more important, God calls all believers to love and serve him and our neighbors in every task we undertake, including our occupations, families, and even hobbies.[28] For the Christian who studies the past, being a historian is a calling.

When we view the occupation of historian as a calling rather than a mere job, it results in a deliberately Christian approach to the historian's work. First, he pursues the study of the past according to the highest standards of the profession, ultimately to glorify God. There should be no such thing as a sloppy Christian historian; we should pursue excellence in our craft as a way to reflect, however finitely, the excellence of our Creator and Lord. Second, he engages in the historical discipline as a humble act of service toward others, including other historians, students, and even casual readers. This can be difficult, especially for those historians who become a part of the historical scholarly community, a guild that is often competitive, insular, and elitist. Finally, he is willing, when applicable, to use his historical training to advance the cause of the gospel, even if this is not his primary calling. I

---

[28] See Gustav Wingren, *Luther on Vocation*, trans. Carl C. Rasmussen (1957; repr., Eugene, OR: Wipf and Stock, 2004).

will address this point in greater detail in the final section of this chapter.[29]

THE NEED FOR "BILINGUAL" CHRISTIAN HISTORIANS

I have tried to make the case that the professional historian can embrace a robustly Christian approach to history without advocating a providentialist paradigm. At this point, some readers may think that I believe there is no place for spiritual interpretations or applications of history. Actually, I am in favor of believing historians interpreting and applying history in an overtly spiritual manner—sometimes. I would argue that one's intended audience should determine how one chooses to engage history. This is especially true when dealing with subjects related to religion or other topics (such as philosophy) that make ultimate claims about the nature of reality and morality. Is it ever appropriate to "preach through history?"[30] Yes, though context will help one to determine when this is the case.

Mark Noll argues that the Christian historian has four tasks: (1) to speak *in* the historical profession by engaging in quality research, writing, and teaching; (2) to speak *to* the profession by demonstrating how the Christian faith influences the work of the historian; (3) to speak *to* the church by providing a more comprehensive, nuanced alternative to simplistically providentialist accounts of history; (4) to speak *in* the church through faithful participation in the body of Christ.[31] I appreciate Noll's approach, but I would expand his fourth task by adding that, when we un-

---

[29] For a helpful essay on understanding history as a calling, see Douglas A. Sweeney, "On the Vocation of Historians to the Priesthood of Believers: A Plea to Christians in the Academy," in *Confessing History: Explorations in Christian Faith and the Historian's Vocation*, eds. John Fea, Jay Green, and Eric Miller (Notre Dame, IN: University of Notre Dame Press, 2010), 299–315. This entire collection of essays is framed around the concept of vocation.

[30] See James B. Lagrand, "The Problems of Preaching through History," in *Confessing History*, eds. Fea, Green, and Miller, 187–213. My own approach differs from that of Lagrand, who rejects the idea that history might have a homiletical use.

[31] Mark A. Noll, "The Conference on Faith and History and the Study of Early American History," *Fides et Historia* 11, no.1 (Fall 1978): 8–18.

derstand that being a historian is a vocation, one of the ways we participate in the body of Christ is by using our historical gifts to build up the church. While part of this certainly entails counter-ing providentialist history, I believe we should also be willing, in certain overtly religious contexts, to offer our humble suggestions (rather than authoritative pronouncements) about how God might have been at work at particular points in history. Furthermore, I think we should be willing—again, in religious settings—to make moral and spiritual application from the past. Christian historians should learn to cultivate "bilingual" instincts because of our "dual calling" as historians who are believers to use our skills to serve both the discipline and the church.[32] I discuss this topic more in the next chapter.

In a helpful essay about the debate over providentialist history, Andrew Atherstone argues that both "confessional" and "profes-sional" history have their legitimate places.[33] I agree. When con-sidering the proper contexts for these two approaches, again the Dutch Reformed tradition offers a helpful resource to Christian historians attempting to navigate this issue. In his classic essay "Sphere Sovereignty," the Dutch Reformed theologian Abraham Kuyper argued that God has ordained differing spheres (domains/sectors) throughout creation to which he has delegated his author-ity, each of which is governed, through common grace, by its own norms, expectations, and responsibilities. Human flourishing is directly tied to acknowledging God's sovereignty over all of life while faithfully living according to the pattern of each sphere.[34] Professional history is part of the sphere of intellectual inquiry in the school or academy rather than the sphere of the church. Con-fessional history is part of the sphere of the church rather than the

---

[32] The language of "dual calling" comes from Robert Tracy McKenzie, "Don't Forget the Church: Reflections on the Forgotten Dimension of Our Dual Calling," in *Confessing History*, eds. Fea, Green, and Miller, 280–98.

[33] Atherstone, "Hagiography and History."

[34] Abraham Kuyper, "Sphere Sovereignty," in *Abraham Kuyper: A Centennial Reader*, ed. James D. Bratt (Grand Rapids, MI: Eerdmans, 1998), 461–90.

sphere of the academy. The "language" a historian chooses to use depends upon the sphere in which she is working.

When a professional historian is speaking to colleagues in the guild, whether through a book, article, or conference paper, he should avoid overtly spiritual interpretations and applications. This is not to say that the school or academy should be free of religion. This Christian historian should be free to share how his faith motivates him and influences his approach to the craft of history; this chapter has suggested a number of ways the Christian worldview affects how one approaches history. His historical work might even open up opportunities for overtly religious conversations based upon questions that are raised by his colleagues or readers. However, since the purpose of professional history is historical inquiry rather than spiritual formation, when speaking to the guild, the Christian historian should speak the "language" of that sphere, though always, of course, being willing to testify to her faith in Christ when appropriate opportunities arise.

When a professional historian speaks to the church, he should be more willing to move in a confessional direction and humbly offer his opinion about how God might have been at work in the past and what it might mean for us today. This should not mean adopting an uncritically providentialist posture; historical rigor and appropriate interpretive nuance should still be brought to bear on the subject. Nevertheless, because the sphere in question is the church rather than the academy, the "language" of the faith is appropriate when invoked in the right way and toward the right ends. The purpose of the church is not intellectual inquiry for its own sake, but rather the proclamation of the gospel to nonbelievers and the spiritual formation of believers.

Christian historians should cultivate a bilingual strategy that enables them to speak to the guild without resorting to providentialism and to the church without pretending as if God were not sovereign over history. To be clear, I am not suggesting any duplicity on the part of a Christian historian; you should not be afraid to tell the academy you are a Christian and you should not be embarrassed to tell other Christians you are a trained historian. Christian integrity should preclude even the hint of any "doublespeak" on the part of a believing historian. Historical bilingualism, rightly practiced, is rooted in a proper understanding of one's immediate context, not an inappropriate desire to hide anything from a particular audience.[35]

A bilingual approach will not always be easy to navigate, even when pursued with absolute integrity. Admittedly, some contexts blur the spheres. An American history class at a Christian college is part of the professional guild, but is probably open to confessional insights. A historical lecture sponsored by a local church takes place in a confessional context, but the audience is likely more open to hearing the insights of a professional historian rather than simply a thoughtful pastor or other ministry leader. Though cultivating historical bilingualism will likely be difficult at times, the hard work is worth the effort as Christian historians seek to honor God in every sphere to which they are called to speak through their gifts. In the next chapter, I will introduce you to many of the spheres— and even subspheres—where a background in history can be of particular use.

---

[35] I am especially grateful to Richard Bailey's incisive critique of an earlier draft of this section, which pointed out the potential dangers of "bilingual" language being misunderstood as some sort of lack of full disclosure or other form of dishonesty. I hope my suggestions are clearer and more helpful based upon the revisions I have made in light of Bailey's comments.

4

HISTORY:
AN INVITATION

But from the late nineteenth century on, when the norm that governed a career in service to history came increasingly to be the creation, transmission, and evaluation of historical learning by specially trained people working full time as historians on college and university faculties, professional history became roughly coterminous with academic history. Yet it is now becoming clear that, rather than being a terminal point in the history of the discipline of history, history's main residence in the academy, although a century long, ought to be considered provisional and, while still the center of gravity in a larger constellation of professional locations, only one among many places from which history has begun to reemerge into the larger society.[1]

James Banner

As I write this chapter, Americans are commemorating the seventieth anniversary of the D-day invasion of June 6, 1944. On that day, over 150,000 Allied soldiers stormed the beaches of Normandy, France, and began the Allied invasion of Germany. Eleven months later, Germany surrendered on May 8, 1945. Japan surrendered four months after Germany on August 15. World War II, the bloodiest war in world history, was finally over. D-day proved to be a decisive turning point in the war. Since that time, Americans have had an endless fascination with D-day. Hundreds of books have been written on the topic, including Stephen Ambrose's narrative history *Band of Brothers* (1992), which was later made into an award-winning

---

[1] James M. Banner Jr., *Being a Historian: An Introduction to the Professional World of History* (New York: Cambridge University Press, 2012), 1–2.

HBO miniseries in 2001.[2] Two Academy Award–winning movies have been made about the battle: *The Longest Day* (1962) and *Saving Private Ryan* (1998). Every year, around one million people visit the Normandy American Cemetery and Memorial, where almost 9400 American soldiers are buried and the names are recorded of another 1557 who were declared "missing in action."[3] This day is a fitting reminder that the past is important because it has profoundly shaped the present. Just think: while millions of people are interested in the past, historians get to spend their lives studying it.

By now, you are well on your way to understanding the discipline of history from the perspective of the Christian intellectual tradition. In the introduction, you were introduced to history and encouraged to think about the discipline from the perspective of the Christian worldview. In subsequent chapters, you have learned about the nature and types of history, the schools of historical interpretation and the importance of historiography, and the oft-debated relationship between faith and history in the life of a believing historian. In this final chapter, I want to invite you to the wonderful world of history. I will begin by arguing that history matters, both for your education and your growth as an individual. I will also suggest several ways that history can be useful for modern men and women. This chapter will also discuss various vocational and occupational routes for which a major or minor in history or a similar field can be particularly helpful. You might be surprised to discover the many different ways that historians can use their training on the other side of their formal education. Whether you become a professional historian or use your historical skills in a different field, I hope you will accept my invitation and become a lifelong student of history.

[2] Stephen E. Ambrose, *Band of Brothers, E Company, 506th Regiment, 101st Airborne: From Normandy to Hitler's Eagle's Nest* (New York: Simon & Schuster, 2001). Following the release of the miniseries, Ambrose's book, which was almost a decade old, became a best seller. It has been reprinted in several editions during subsequent years.

[3] Information taken from the website of the Normandy American Cemetery and Memorial, accessed June 6, 2014, http://www.abmc.gov/cemeteries-memorials/europe/normandy-american-cemetery.

HISTORY MATTERS

History matters, perhaps in more ways than you realize. Of course, history matters when it comes to your education, even if you are not a history major or minor. Many colleges and universities emphasize the liberal arts as part of their core curriculums. According to Gene Fant, "Liberal learning, sometimes called the liberal arts (as distinct from the practical arts), aimed at a breadth of knowledge that included a wide range of subjects that trained the mind to analyze challenges and formulate solutions or to anticipate opportunities and strategies."[4] The idea of the liberal arts began in ancient Greece, was refined by the Romans, and then "baptized" by the Christian intellectual tradition during the Middle Ages. The most important figure in wedding the liberal arts to the Christian worldview was Alcuin of York (735–804), a scholar-monk and the architect of the "Carolingian Renaissance" during the reign of Charlemagne in western Europe. The seven classical liberal arts included the *trivium* of grammar, logic, and rhetoric, and the *quadrivium* of arithmetic, astronomy, music, and geometry. The liberal arts animated the educational vision of the great monasteries of medieval Europe. Today, many Christian private schools, colleges, and home educators have attempted to recover the classical liberal arts and apply them to the modern world.[5]

While there have always been chroniclers of history, the study of history was not one of the classical liberal arts. As we discussed in chapter 2, history as a distinct discipline only emerged in the nineteenth century as the academic world became more focused upon specialization. Nevertheless, as James Patterson notes,

---

[4] Gene C. Fant Jr., *The Liberal Arts: A Student's Guide*, Reclaiming the Christian Intellectual Tradition (Wheaton, IL: Crossway, 2012), 24–25.

[5] The key event that rekindled Christian interest in a classical liberal arts education was Dorothy Sayers's 1947 address "The Lost Tools of Learning," which has been reprinted many times and is available widely on the Internet. For example, see http://www.gbt.org/text/sayers.html (accessed June 3, 2014). For a leading proponent of the classical liberal arts among evangelicals, see Douglas Wilson, *Recovering the Lost Tools of Learning: An Approach to Distinctively Christian Education*, Turning Point Christian Worldview Series (Wheaton, IL: Crossway, 1991); and Wilson, *The Case for Classical Christian Education* (Wheaton, IL: Crossway, 2003).

"current cultural and societal expectations suggest that a truly educated person will have studied history in some format."[6] Thus, though history was not part of the *trivium* or the *quadrivium*, it is normally considered to be part of a modern liberal arts education. Middle school and high school students normally study American history, European history, some world history, and the history of their respective state. In most colleges and universities, students are required to take at least some courses in American history, world history, and/or Western civilization as part of their core curriculum requirements. Of course, many colleges and universities also offer majors or minors in history, history education, and related fields. More than likely, you are currently reading this book because you are majoring or minoring in a historical field.

More broadly, history matters in that it helps to form us into mature, responsible, well-rounded individuals. Patterson suggests six reasons why the study of history is beneficial, regardless of one's major or one's ultimate occupational goals. First, familiarity with history contributes to the modern concept of a good education. A sense of historical consciousness is a crucial component in being an educated individual. Second, history is a necessary ingredient in the formation of our individual and corporate identity. We best understand ourselves, and the institutions with which we identify, when we appreciate how we relate to the past. Third, historical knowledge nurtures and reinforces cultural knowledge. We best understand our culture when we appreciate how it relates to the past. Fourth, history provides a vast amount of information about human experience that offers the potential for contemporary application. It is appropriate and even advisable to mine the past for contemporary application, especially for believing historians who are convinced that all truth is God's truth. Fifth, a sense of historical awareness usually makes for better citizens, especially for

---

[6] James A. Patterson, "The Study of History," in *Faith and Learning: A Handbook for Christian Higher Education*, ed. David S. Dockery (Nashville: B&H Academic, 2012), 219.

those who live in a representative democracy like the United States. Historical understanding is a key ingredient in an informed electorate. Finally, students of history soon discover that many historians and biographers write insightful, even entertaining, historical literature. Simply put, many people enjoy reading and learning from history.[7]

History also matters because it can be very useful in helping us to think wisely and live faithfully and fruitfully in the present. I have suggested at points throughout this book that the study of the past is a virtue unto itself. It is a good thing for historians to seek to understand the past and make it understandable to contemporary audiences, whether in the classroom, the courtroom, the sanctuary, or the reading club. But history also offers us many useful applications. As Marc Bloch argues in his classic textbook *The Historian's Craft*, "it is undeniable that a science will always seem to us somehow incomplete if it cannot, sooner or later, in one way or another, aid us to live better."[8] It seems unlikely that most historians will ever again understand their discipline to be a subdiscipline of theology or philosophy; for better or worse, history is a stand-alone discipline with its own guild, conventions, and assumptions. To be clear, this need not mean that historians, and especially Christian historians, should drink too deeply from the secular worldview that coincided with the rise and development of professional history. History can and should *move* us at times.

Historians sometimes express hesitancy about efforts to apply the past to the present, and for good reason. As you will remember from the first chapter, in American culture at least both conservatives and liberals politicize history when they interpret the past through the lens of their agendas and then appropriate historical insights to advance those agendas in the public square. Furthermore, the greater the emphasis one places on the usefulness of

---

[7] Ibid., 219–22.
[8] Marc Bloch, *The Historian's Craft* (New York: Alfred A. Knopf, 1953; repr., Manchester, England, UK: Manchester University Press, 1992), 9.

history, the greater the temptation to embrace presentist interpretations of the past. Nevertheless, as James Banner argues, professional historians have almost always seen the value in reaching outside of the academy and engaging the general public in an effort to provide a "usable past" to various audiences. Indeed, most historians have been interested in "conveying historical knowledge to the general public, influencing governmental, industrial, and commercial policies, and maintaining history's role in the schools."[9]

Though we must be cautious in applying the past to the present, Christian historians in particular, with our belief in the doctrines of providence and common grace, should not hesitate to offer contemporary prescription from our study of history. Though history is primarily a descriptive discipline, historians should never be so clinically detached from the world that we refuse to ever offer any prescription based upon our knowledge of the past. However, we should always make prescriptive application with an attitude of humility, understanding that interpretations and applications of history are always provisional. As we learned in the last chapter, it is not always easy to discern God's hand in human history, and even when we think we know what God was up to, we never have comprehensive knowledge of God's past (or present) providence.

One reason we should not totally avoid historical prescription is because the past casts a long shadow over the present. John Fea contends that the past has shaped every person who is alive today. Because the past is a part of who we are, even when we do not realize it, he suggests several ways that history is relevant to the present.[10] The past is useful to us as a source of inspiration as we learn from those who have gone before us. Christian historians in particular have often been willing to study the past for the sake of inspiration, especially when teaching or writing for a believing audience. The past is also beneficial because it provides an escape

---

[9] Banner, *Being a Historian*, 24.
[10] John Fea, *Why Study History? Reflecting on the Importance of the Past* (Grand Rapids, MI: Baker Academic, 2013), 30–42.

from the pressures and anxieties of our lives. Like a good movie (especially a historical movie!), sometimes it is a healthy thing to enjoy the past for the sake of entertainment and, perhaps, some needed perspective.[11] The past is also helpful in that it reminds us who we are. As individuals, we each have roots that have molded us in more ways than we realize. The same is true of institutions, local communities, and entire nations. For Christians, the past has played a crucial role in shaping our religious identity; we are inheritors of "the faith that was once for all delivered to the saints" (Jude 3). Fea reminds us that, "If you are a historian, part of your responsibility is to inform the general public about the way the past connects to our contemporary lives and to help members of your community use the past to make meaning of their lives."[12] All good historians, but especially Christian historians, should be committed to the belief that the past matters in a variety of different ways.

HISTORY BEYOND COLLEGE OR UNIVERSITY

Colleges and universities offer a variety of majors and minors related to history. Of course, many schools have undergraduate degree programs in history and history education. Some schools offer more specialized majors. For example, some schools that cater to military personnel offer a major in military history. Some Christian schools offer a major in church history or history of Christianity. Many schools, especially those with a larger history department, offer concentrations within the broader discipline of history. Common specializations include American history, European history, military history, religious history, Southern history, global history, and public history. Even when a school does not offer official concentrations, in many cases students carve out specializations based upon the elective courses they take. In my own undergraduate program, though we did not have concentrations, nearly all of

---

[11] Bloch makes a similar point when he speaks of the "entertainment value" of history. See Bloch, *The Historian's Craft*, 6.
[12] Fea, *Why Study History?*, 46.

my electives were in either Southern history or military history. (The college actually added a concentration in "Southern Studies" a couple of years after I graduated.)

So what are the postgraduation options for a young historian beyond the bachelor's degree? Before discussing the many options available to you, it is worth briefly revisiting the doctrine of vocation, which we introduced in the previous chapter.[13] In the Christian intellectual tradition, and especially among Protestants, we have a long history of arguing that the Lord has given various callings or vocations to every believer. Your eventual occupation, though important, is only one of these vocations. Other vocations include whether or not God is calling you to be married and raise children, specific types of service he is calling you to, both through and outside of your local church involvement, even particular hobbies. The doctrine of vocation is ultimately behind all of our roles, responsibilities, and pursuits. For example, God has called me to be a follower of Jesus Christ; a husband to Leah; a father to Georgia, Baxter, Eleanor, and Fuller; a professor; a minister; a son; a brother; a citizen; and an author. He has called you to similar, though not identical, vocations. The Lord has blessed each of us with natural talents, cultivated abilities, spiritual gifts, and opportunities to pursue those callings in a way that brings glory to him and that serves other people. In God's common grace, much of this is also true for unbelievers, even if they do not acknowledge that their desires, talents, and opportunities ultimately come from the Lord. Non-Christians often feel a deep sense of calling to their vocations, though they do not normally think of calling in a religious sense.

As with every discipline of study, for many individuals their academic study of history factors into their vocations as they seek to use their training in pursuing God's plan for their occupations,

---

[13] For a helpful contemporary introduction to the Protestant doctrine of vocation, see Gene Edward Veith, *God at Work: Your Christian Vocation in All of Life* (Wheaton, IL: Crossway, 2011).

families, spiritual life, hobbies, and service to others. Before you consider what direction to go after graduation, you should attempt to discern what vocations you believe the Lord has called you to and how the study of history might factor into the faithful pursuing of those vocations. If you are uncertain what vocations the Lord is calling you to pursue, it is worth talking about these matters with your parents, spouse (if applicable), pastors, professors, guidance counselors, and other wise and hopefully godly individuals. In the case of each of these individuals, part of their vocation is to help you discern your vocation.

Once you have a sense of your vocation(s), it becomes a bit easier to think of how to apply your study of history to life after graduation. You have likely chosen your major with a particular vocation in view. For example, most individuals who major in history education do so with the intention of teaching history in a public or private middle school or high school. Some folks who major in history also do so unto this end. Many private schools do not require an education degree; a bachelor of arts in history is often sufficient. Some states also allow individuals to teach in public schools without an education degree, provided that they are willing to be certified, take some additional courses in the field of education, or earn a master's degree in education, teaching, or a similar field. For example, the GaTapp program helps individuals without an education degree to secure teaching posts in public schools and receive the additional training that they need to pursue that vocation with excellence.[14]

Another common postgraduation option for history majors is graduate school. The sort of graduate school depends upon one's sense of calling. Not surprisingly, many history majors are called to pursue graduate work in history. Sometimes they opt for a master's degree in history as a terminal degree. More often, professional historians pursue a PhD in history. If a student's undergraduate

---

[14] You can learn about GaTapp at https://www.gapsc.com/EducatorPreparation/GaTAPP/GaTAPP.aspx.

program did not offer concentrations, it is at this stage that a student will narrow his interests to a particular region, sub-discipline, and, often, type of history. For example, he might focus on British history, specializing in the history of the women's suffrage movement in the early twentieth century, studying it from the perspective of social history. Earning a PhD in history can prepare you for a number of vocations, including college or university teaching, full-time research (often for the government or a think tank), museum curation, public history (more below), or professional editing. A growing number of historians with PhDs work full-time in a field unrelated to history, but teach part-time at a local college or university. Due to the shrinking job market for full-time history professors (and professors in other disciplines), these numbers will likely continue to grow in the future.[15]

Another common vocation among history majors is public history. Public history is the use of professional history outside of the academy, most often in public institutions such as museums, libraries, archives, historical societies, and government agencies. For example, some former history majors work as tour guides or researchers for a Revolutionary War or Civil War battlefield, the birthplace of a famous individual, a local museum, or a historic district or history-themed attraction. Others work as the official historians or archivists for various companies, government agencies, or any number of other institutions. Many history majors work as park rangers for the National Park Service. While it is often not necessary to earn an additional degree to work in public history, as with many occupations, the more specialized training you have, in general the better the job you can find. Numerous schools offer graduate programs in public history.[16] As an aside,

---

[15] See L. Maren Wood, "What Doors Does a Ph.D. in History Open?," *The Chronicle of Higher Education*, October 30, 2012, accessed June 5, 2014, http://chronicle.com/article/What-Doors-Does-a-PhD-in/135448/.

[16] For more on the field of public history, see the website for the National Council on Public History at http://ncph.org/cms/.

even if you become an academic historian, look for ways to dabble in public history and make your work accessible for those beyond your classroom and your fellow historians.[17]

Many individuals who major or minor in history do not want to be professional historians, but rather want to be historically informed as they pursue a different vocation. Fortunately, history teaches you many skills that are valuable in a number of different careers: formulating a research topic, advancing a written argument, understanding the difference between primary and secondary sources, and being able to express your thoughts clearly in writing. John Fea lists a number of famous people who studied history but who are not professional historians, including two former presidents of the United States, two Supreme Court justices, a movie producer, several elected politicians, several news anchors and other members of the media, well-known actors, famous professional athletes, accomplished businesspeople, and even an astronaut![18] I would add to Fea's list a former secretary of state (Henry Kissinger), two best-selling authors (Ayn Rand and Malcolm Gladwell), a Grammy Award–winning singer-songwriter (Lauryn Hill), hundreds of pastors and other ministry leaders, and loads of homeschooling mothers and fathers.[19]

I will briefly mention several occupations besides being a professional historian where a background in history can be especially helpful. Many history majors finish their undergraduate program and enter law school. Anecdotally, it is common to hear that more

---

[17] For helpful essays on the importance of academic historians being willing to engage in public history and even writing for a more popular audience, see John Lukacs, "Popular and Professional History," in *Recent Themes in Historical Thinking: Historians in Conversation*, ed. Donald A. Yerxa (Columbia, SC: University of South Carolina Press, 2008), 44–50; and Jeremy Black, "The Public Use of History," in *Recent Themes in Historical Thinking: Historians in Conversation*, ed. Donald A. Yerxa (Columbia, SC: University of South Carolina Press, 2008), 51–54.

[18] Fea, *Why Study History?*, 143. This section of Fea's book is adapted from his personal blog, which has been running a series titled "What Can You Do With a History Major?" since 2009. See John Fea, *The Way of Improvement Leads Home* (blog), accessed October 3, 2014, http://www.philipvickersfithian.com/. At the time of this writing, Fea's series extends to fifty posts.

[19] For lists of well-known history majors who are not professional historians, see the websites for the history departments at University of Illinois (http://www.history.illinois.edu/undergraduate/history/) and Bethel University (http://cas.bethel.edu/dept/history/famous_majors).

history majors apply to law school than pursue graduate studies in history. This makes perfect sense; the skills one acquires as a history major, when coupled with good oral communication skills, offer the ideal academic background for a would-be lawyer. As mentioned already, two of the current justices on the United States Supreme Court, Antonin Scalia and Sonia Sotomayor, were history majors. Several of my fellow history majors in college were planning to apply to law school. One of my wife's good friends from college was a history major who went on to study at a prestigious regional law school. He has served as an assistant district attorney and is currently the managing partner of a law firm in North Georgia. Of course, not everyone who majors in history and then earns a law degree spends his whole career as a lawyer. Erick Erickson, the editor-in-chief of the influential conservative website RedState.com, studied history and political science as an undergrad, earned a law degree, and practiced law for a few years before beginning his career as a political commentator.

Many history majors go on to work in libraries. This is also a natural fit; if you like history, you probably like books, and if you like books, you probably like libraries. Librarians who work in an academic setting are often required to have expertise in a particular subject; many of them have backgrounds in history. Even in settings where a specialization is not required, the research and organizational skills acquired in a history program are great preparation for serving as a librarian. In general, to be a full-time librarian in an academic institution or a public library you need to earn a master of library science degree. In addition to librarians, archivists often work in, or closely with, libraries. Archivists manage records and preserve collections of various materials for all sorts of institutions. Think about it like this: archivists are the gatekeepers for the primary sources that historians need to conduct their research. An archivist might work for an academic institution, a government agency, a historical society, or even a business. As with librarians, career archivists in academic settings normally need to earn a master of library science degree, but with specialization in archival studies. While I was pursuing my graduate studies, I worked for four years in the archives of two different schools, serving as both a part-time archival assistant and eventually a full-time salaried associate archivist.

Some history majors become documentary filmmakers. This is especially the case for historians who specialize in oral history, which is the collection and study of the past through such sources as audio-visual materials, transcriptions, and interviews.[20] Obviously, majoring in history alone will not prepare you to be a filmmaker. You need to also learn the craft of filmmaking, build appropriate connections in the filmmaking industry, and unless you are independently wealthy, learn how to raise funds and secure sponsors for potential projects. However, if you can gain these skills and experiences, a background in history can be an asset in researching a topic, writing a script, and telling an engaging narrative. Stephen Ives is one of the most successful documentary filmmakers in America. Ives began his career working with Ken Burns, who is arguably the most famous documentary filmmaker working today. Since the early 1990s, Ives has produced and directed a number of films including *The West* (1996), *Reporting America at War* (2003), *Road to Memphis* (2010), and *Constitution USA* (2013). His 2003 documentary *Seabiscuit*, part of PBS's acclaimed American Experience series, won a Primetime Emmy Award. Prior to embarking upon a career making documentaries, Ives majored in American history as an undergraduate at Harvard University.

A final vocation for many history majors is full-time Christian ministry. If you earn a degree in history, hopefully you will learn how to interpret the past, read critically, and argue a thesis in writing. These are helpful skills for pastors and other ministry leaders who are called to teach the Bible and pass on the best of

---

[20] See the website for the Oral History Association, http://www.oralhistory.org/.

the Christian intellectual tradition to others. Many history majors graduate from college and pursue graduate studies at a seminary or divinity school. As a former seminary professor, I have taught many dozens of students who have told me they majored in history as undergrads. Almost to a student, they find that their background in history has well prepared them for their classes in Old Testament, New Testament, theology, ethics, philosophy, and, of course, church history. Beyond seminary, many ministers have found that being students of the past is very helpful when it comes to leading a congregation or parachurch ministry, preaching thoughtful and relevant sermons, and teaching Christian doctrine and ethics to those to whom they are called to minister.

Some who are called to full-time vocational ministry will decide to pursue advanced graduate work in disciplines such as church history, theology, ethics, or philosophy. Some will earn a PhD in one of these fields and become a professor in a seminary, a Christian studies department at a college or university, or a Bible college. Others will teach and train Christian leaders in foreign mission contexts. Still others will be pastor-scholars who will use their advanced training to strengthen their ministry of teaching and perhaps writing. This is my testimony. I majored in history and minored in Christian studies as an undergraduate. As a senior in college, I wrestled with whether or not I wanted to pursue an MA in history or an MDiv at a theological seminary. After a season of prayer and seeking counsel from some trusted advisors, I opted for the latter. Following my master's studies, I earned a PhD in church history. For several years I taught the history of Christianity to both undergraduates and graduates at a theological seminary. I have no doubt I am a far better *church* historian because of my undergraduate training as a historian.

As you can see, there is no single way to be a historian. In fact, historians have never had as much freedom as they do now to pursue a variety of different occupations, many of which do not involve classrooms, journal articles, monographs, or formal lectures. As you decide what it means for you to use your historical training in the future, consider one last piece of advice that I have adapted from the insights of James Banner: be yourself as a historian.[21] Follow your instincts, whatever they may be, about the historical subjects that most interest you. Pursue occupations and even hobbies that fit with your curiosities, temperament, abilities, and opportunities. Seek input from others, pray for wisdom from the Lord, then begin to find your way as a historian, whatever that might mean in your particular situation. As Polonius said to Laertes in Shakespeare's *Hamlet*, "This above all: to thine own self be true."

HISTORY AND THE LOCAL CHURCH

Since this is a book written primarily for Christian undergraduate students who are interested in studying history, I need to introduce you to one more way you can use a major or minor in history. Chances are, many of you reading this book are members of local churches and/or active in various sorts of Christian ministries and activities. Whether you become a professional historian or use your historical training in some other occupation, there is also perhaps a place for you to use your background for the benefit of your local church, Bible study, or parachurch ministry. I touched on this briefly in the last chapter, though the focus was upon the legitimate role of "confessional" history in overtly religious contexts. In this section, I want to focus a bit more on serving the body of Christ through the ministry of history.

Many Christians are woefully ignorant of the past, even the Christian past. What they do know about the past is often cobbled together from half-remembered history classes from middle school and high school, partisan comments from political commentators, and popular history books that are frequently driven by the same

---

[21] Banner, *Being a Historian*, 250–51.

political agendas advocated by the commentators. This is especially the case when it comes to the question of the role of Christianity in America's history, a topic we discussed in the previous chapter. As a general rule, Christian publishers publish relatively few books that discuss historical topics and are written for a general Christian audience. Yet, like Americans in general, American Christians are often at least interested in history, as evidenced through their reading of popular biographies and narrative histories and watching programs on the History channel. As you become a trained historian, I would encourage you to find ways to help your fellow Christians think in more thoughtful ways about history.

In a helpful essay titled "Don't Forget the Church," Robert Tracy McKenzie suggests that Christian historians have a dual calling to serve both the historical academy and the body of Christ: "I have come to believe that, as a Christian historian, I am called not only to labor within the academy as a Christian, but also to labor within the church as a historian."[22] McKenzie then recommends seven ways that historians can use their skills in service to the church. First, he suggests beginning with your own local church by finding ways to teach your fellow church members about history. Second, he argues historians need to make a positive case for the importance of history. (Hopefully, this book can help you to do that.) Third, you should strive to eliminate unnecessary boundaries by speaking in a way and at a level that general Christian audiences can understand. Fourth, you must learn the interests of your target audience and familiarize yourself with their concerns so that you can helpfully address them. Fifth, you should learn the objectives of your audience and take them seriously. To what degree are they interested in history? Why is that the case and how can you help them grow in their historical awareness? Sixth, you should

---

[22] Robert Tracy McKenzie, "Don't Forget the Church: Reflections on the Forgotten Dimension of Our Dual Calling," in *Confessing History: Explorations in Christian Faith and the Historian's Vocation*, eds. John Fea, Jay Green, and Eric Miller (Notre Dame, IN: University of Notre Dame Press, 2010), 280.

search proactively for common ground with your audience, seeking to affirm as many of their presuppositions as possible, even as you sometimes try to point them to a better way. Finally, and most importantly, you must strive to love the church as you attempt to help Christians think about the nature and purposes of history.[23] I would expand on this last point by suggesting that one way for historians to love God and love their neighbor is by lovingly using their historical training to equip the body of Christ.

Building upon some of the suggestions of McKenzie and Fea, as well as my own experiences, I will close by suggesting some concrete ways you can serve local churches in particular with your historical training. To be clear, I well understand you will probably not be able to serve in some of these ways right now; most college students do not have the time or opportunity to teach in their local churches. However, at some point you may have the occasion and inclination to take some of these suggestions to heart. Start planning today for how you might use your knowledge of history to bless your church in the future.

First of all, consider developing a Sunday school class on the history of Christianity. In my own local church, I have taught a thirteen-week survey of Christian history several times. People need to know their roots, and this is especially true of those who are part of the body of Christ. Second, consider forming a history-themed reading group in your local congregation. You can either read works related to church history or you can read books on general historical topics and help the group to think Christianly about the subject covered in the book. Third, if your church includes homeschooling families, consider teaching or tutoring homeschooled students on topics related to history. Fourth, consider asking your pastor or staff to sponsor occasional lectures by you or other historians on topics that would be of interest to believers. You can invite

---

[23] Ibid., 280–95. Fea makes a similar case to McKenzie, but with emphasis on the "Christian America" question. See Fea, *Why Study History?*, 158–71.

believing historians to visit your church and distill their research in a way that everyday Christians can understand and appreciate. These are a handful of suggestions that come to mind; there are likely many other ways you can promote historical awareness in a local church. Be as creative as you can and pray that the Lord of all history would give you the wisdom to own the vocation of being a historian in service to the church.

CONCLUSION

It is time for me to conclude this chapter and this book. I hope you agree that history is a noble discipline that is worth pursuing. God is sovereign over every past, present, and future event. He calls historians, whether professional or not, to help interpret the past for those living in the present. Hopefully, many of you who are reading this book will accept the invitation to become a professional historian and use your training to help others to understand the past. Even if you choose not to pursue a path where you are paid to study, teach, and/or write about the past, I trust you will find many ways to use your historical training to benefit yourself and others in whatever vocation(s) you ultimately choose. Finally, for those of you reading this book who have been "on the fence" about this whole history thing, I hope I have helped convince you that history matters to God and it should matter to you, even if you choose a different major and future career path.

QUESTIONS FOR REFLECTION

1) What is the relationship between the past and history? What possible errors arise when we confuse these two concepts?

2) "All historians are revisionists because all historians are doing their best to interpret some aspect of the past with the best source material available to them" (p. 28). Do you agree or disagree with this statement? If you disagree, what is the reason for your disagreement?

3) What is presentism? Why does it pose such a danger for historians? What are some of the more common forms of presentism you have observed?

4) What is the Judeo-Christian interpretation of history? How does it contrast with other influential approaches to history?

5) What is the relationship between a historian's faith and how he or she interprets history? Is there a way to teach or write about religious history without resorting to providentialist interpretations? Is it ever appropriate to make contemporary spiritual or moral application based upon the past?

6) In what ways does a Christian worldview affect the way a historian interprets the past? What are some particular resources from the Christian intellectual tradition that are especially helpful to historians?

7) What are some of the vocations where formal historical training can be useful besides being a professional historian?

GLOSSARY

Common grace. Grace that does not affect one's salvation and that is common to all humankind, whether Christians or non-Christians.

Cultural history. Incorporates insights from anthropology into historical inquiry to examine popular cultural traditions and cultural interpretations of historical experiences.

Cyclical history. History is a series of endlessly repeating cycles without any beginning or ending and with no ultimate meaning.

Declension narrative. History that recounts a falling away from an earlier ideal.

Diplomatic history. The study of international relations between various nation-states in the past.

Economic history. The study of economic theories and trends among individuals, movements, or civilizations in the past.

Environmental history. The study of human interaction with the natural world in the past.

The fall. Adam and Eve's original sin in the garden of Eden which resulted in the sinfulness of all their natural descendants and the distortion of the created order from God's original intention.

Gender history. The study of gender-related phenomena in the past.

General revelation. Includes the various ways that God discloses knowledge of himself through natural means, including nature and conscience.

Historical fallacy. Erroneous logical reasoning that leads to incorrect interpretations of the past regardless of the validity of the sources used.

Historicism. All cultures are determined by their histories, therefore the past should be interpreted differently in each culture because every culture is unique and thus developing in its own peculiar way.

Historiography. The study of changes over time in the methods, interpretations, and conclusions of previous historians.

History. The discipline of reconstructing and interpreting the past.

History as progress. The historical process is linear and human beings are the central players in a world that is ever evolving from a more primitive past.

Imago dei. The doctrine that all human beings are created in God's image and thus possess an inherent dignity and sanctity.

Intellectual history. The study of ideas, arguments, beliefs, assumptions, and attitudes of individuals, movements, or civilizations in the past.

Judeo-Christian history. Historical progression is a linear process that was initiated by God at creation, is ultimately controlled by God, and will reach its conclusion according to God's sovereign plan.

Marxist history. Human beings, and especially "the common man," create the historical process as they labor to satisfy their basic needs.

Military history. The study of phenomena related to armed conflicts between human beings in the past.

Monograph. A book-length essay that studies a specialized topic.

Past. Events that occurred prior to this particular moment in time.

Plagiarism. Using the ideas or words of others without clearly acknowledging the source of information.

Peer review. Subjecting historical interpretations to the scrutiny of other scholars with expertise on the subject being studied.

Presentism. Any attempt to read present assumptions back into the past.

Primary sources. Firsthand materials that come directly from a past individual or institution from the period being studied.

Providence. God's sustaining, guiding, and protecting of his created order by his sovereign power and according to his sovereign plan.

Providentialist history. The task of the historian is to discern God's guiding hand in the events of history.

Religious history. The study of religious individuals, ideas, practices, institutions, traditions, and other related phenomena in the past.

Revisionist history. The reinterpretation of received, popular, or prominent understandings of history, which could be understood either positively or negatively by others.

Secondary sources. The works of other scholars who have studied a particular historical subject.

Secularization thesis. The theory that religion decreases in proportion to the modernization of a society.

Social history. Incorporating insights from social sciences into historical inquiry to study the experiences of ordinary people in the past.

Special revelation. Includes the various ways that God discloses knowledge of himself through supernatural means, including miracles, prophesies, and the inspired Scriptures.

Sphere sovereignty. Doctrine associated with the Dutch Reformed theologian Abraham Kuyper that claims God has ordained differing spheres (domains/sectors) throughout creation to which he has delegated his authority, each of which is governed, through common grace, by its own norms, expectations, and responsibilities.

Vocatio. The doctrine that God is active in every occupation, every station in life, every responsibility, and when these different vocations or callings are undertaken out of love for God and neighbor, the Lord's work is being done in each unique context.

Whig interpretation. A form of presentism, first identified by Herbert Butterfield, that assumes the present is more progressive, enlightened, and/or better than the past and interprets the former based upon these assumptions.

RESOURCES FOR FURTHER STUDY

Augustine. *The City of God (De Civitate Dei), Books 1–10*. Edited by Boniface Ramsey. Translated by William Babcock. Hyde Park, NY: New City, 2012.

———. *The City of God (De Civitate Dei), Books 11–22*. Edited by Boniface Ramsey. Translated by William Babcock. Hyde Park, NY: New City, 2013.

Banner, James M., Jr. *Being a Historian: An Introduction to the Professional World of History*. New York: Cambridge University Press, 2012.

Bebbington, David. *Patterns in History: A Christian Perspective on Historical Thought*. Nottingham, UK: Inter-Varsity, 1979. Reprinted, Vancouver, British Columbia: Regent College Publishing, 1990.

Bede. *The Ecclesiastical History of the English People*. New York: Oxford University Press, 1999.

Bendroth, Margaret. *The Spiritual Practice of Remembering*. Grand Rapids, MI: Eerdmans, 2013.

Breisach, Ernst, ed. *Historiography: Ancient, Medieval, and Modern*. 3rd ed. Chicago: University of Chicago Press, 2007.

Butterfield, Herbert. *Christianity and History*. London: Bell and Sons, 1949.

———. *The Whig Interpretation of History*. New York: Charles Scribner's Sons, 1931.

Dawson, Christopher. *Religion and the Rise of Western Culture*. London: Sheed & Ward, 1950.

Dockery, David S., ed. *Faith and Learning: A Handbook for Christian Higher Education*. Nashville: B&H Academic, 2012.

Eusebius. *The Church History*. Edited and translated by Paul L. Maier. Grand Rapids, MI: Kregel Academic, 2007.

Fea, John. *Was America Founded as a Christian Nation?* Louisville, KY: Westminster-John Knox, 2011.

———. *Why Study History? Reflecting on the Importance of the Past*. Grand Rapids, MI: Baker Academic, 2013.

Fea, John, Jay Green, and Eric Miller, eds. *Confessing History: Explorations in Christian Faith and the Historian's Vocation*. Notre Dame, IN: University of Notre Dame Press, 2010.

Fischer, David Hackett. *Historians' Fallacies: Toward a Logic of Historical Thought*. New York: Harper and Row, 1970.

Gaddis, John Lewis. *The Landscape of History: How Historians Map the Past*. New York: Oxford University Press, 2002.

Goheen, Michael W., and Craig G. Bartholomew. *Living at the Crossroads: An Introduction to Christian Worldview*. Grand Rapids, MI: Baker Academic, 2008.

Keillor, Steven J. *God's Judgments: Interpreting History and the Christian Faith*. Downers Grove, IL: IVP Academic, 2007.

Kuklick, Bruce, and D. G. Hart, eds. *Religious Advocacy and American History*. Grand Rapids, MI: Eerdmans, 1997.

Lowenthal, David. *The Past Is a Foreign Country*. Cambridge and New York: Cambridge University Press, 1985.

Marsden, George M. *The Outrageous Idea of Christian Scholarship*. New York: Oxford University Press, 1997.

Marsden, George M., and Frank Roberts, eds. *A Christian View of History?* Grand Rapids, MI: Eerdmans, 1975.

McIntire, C. T., ed. *Herbert Butterfield: Writings on Christianity and History*. New York: Oxford University Press, 1979.

McIntire, C. T., and Ronald A. Wells, eds. *History and Historical Understanding*. Grand Rapids, MI: Eerdmans, 1984.

Montgomery, John Warwick. *The Shape of the Past: A Christian Response to Secular Philosophies of History*. 2nd ed. Minneapolis: Bethany House, 1975.

Noll, Mark A. *The Scandal of the Evangelical Mind*. Grand Rapids, MI: Eerdmans, 1995.

Ream, Todd C., Jerry Pattengale, and David L. Riggs, eds. *Beyond Integration? Inter/Disciplinary Possibilities for the Future of Christian Higher Education*. Abilene, TX: Abilene Christian University Press, 2012.

Ryken, Philip Graham. *Christian Worldview: A Student's Guide*. Reclaiming the Christian Intellectual Tradition. Wheaton, IL: Crossway, 2013.

Trueman, Carl R. *Histories and Fallacies: Problems Faced in the Writing of History*. Wheaton, IL: Crossway, 2010.

Wells, Ronald A., ed. *History and the Christian Historian*. Grand Rapids, MI: Eerdmans, 1998.

Wilsey, John D. *One Nation under God? An Evangelical Critique of Christian America*. Eugene, OR: Pickwick, 2011.

Wolters, Albert M. *Creation Regained: Biblical Basics for a Reformational Worldview*. 2nd ed. Grand Rapids, MI: Eerdmans, 2005.

Wood, Gordon S. *The Purpose of the Past: Reflections on the Uses of History*. New York: Penguin, 2008.

GENERAL INDEX

SCRIPTURE INDEX

CHECK OUT THE OTHER BOOKS IN THE **RECLAIMING THE CHRISTIAN INTELLECTUAL TRADITION SERIES**

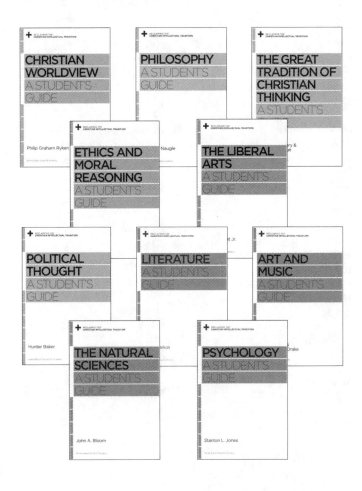

For more information, visit crossway.org.